RENEWING THE EARTH

DEVELOPMENT FOR A SUSTAINABLE FUTURE

D1434562

RENEWING THE EARTH

DEVELOPMENT
FOR A
SUSTAINABLE
FUTURE

An Economic Perspective
Seamus Cleary

CAFOD

The Catholic Fund for Overseas Development
2 Romero Close, Stockwell Road,
London SW9 9TY, England.

CAFOD is the official overseas development agency of the Catholic Church in England and Wales.

First published 1989.

British Library Cataloguing in Publication Data
Cleary, Seamus
   Renewing the earth: development for a sustainable future:
   an economic perspective.
   1. Developing countries. Environment. Effects of
   development projects financed by international development
   agencies
   I. Title II. Catholic Fund for Overseas Development
   304.2'09172'4

ISBN 1-871549-09-4

Designed by David Walker, Ikon Designs.
Typeset, printed and bound in Great Britain by
The Russell Press, Nottingham.

Cover pictures:
1. The western Sahara, *background,* (Roger Hutchings/NETWORK)
2. T-shirted Penan protesters campaigning against the destruction of the forests in Sarawak, Borneo, *inset,* (Nigel Dickinson)
3. Women workers in paddy field, Indonesia, *inset,* (Sean Sprague/CAFOD)

CONTENTS

FOREWORD

The new three-year education campaign, *Renewing the Earth*, reaffirms the commitment of CAFOD (the Catholic Fund for Overseas Development) to the full realisation of human potential throughout the world. In its pursuit of this objective, CAFOD has constantly to grapple with the conflict of interests to which the political, economic and social inequalities between people the world over give rise.

Third world partners constantly stress that CAFOD's response must recognise and integrate all aspects of their experience if this realisation is to be successfully achieved through the expression of Christian solidarity.

The education campaign, which is one way through which CAFOD attempts to express this Christian solidarity, is based on a process of experience, analysis, reflection and action. As a contribution to that process, this book analyses the theme of the campaign, development and the environment, in the light of development economics.

In so doing it makes what we believe is a timely and vital contribution to current debate on the topic. In its report, *Our Common Future* (the Bruntland report, as it came to be known), the World Commission on Environment and Development emphasised the urgent need for policies which respond positively to the global environmental crisis. But it also drew attention to the inadequacy of existing analysis. CAFOD hopes that this book will supply at least something of what is lacking.

The various drafts of the text have benefited from the comments and suggestions of many people, and although it would be impossible to mention them here individually, we wish to express our deep appreciation of the time and care they took. The final text has been considerably improved thanks to their efforts, and any errors which remain are the responsibility of the author alone.

Seamus Cleary
Research Officer
CAFOD, April 1989

CHAPTER 1

INTRODUCTION

In January 1988 torrential rains in Brazil resulted in significant loss of life and extensive physical damage in the city of Rio de Janeiro. Sweeping through the *favelas* (shanty towns) on the steep surrounding slopes, the accumulated water and rubbish destroyed individual homes before going on to threaten the modern apartment blocks in the city below. When the storm was over the city counted 290 dead, 734 injured and 13,943 homeless; and the financial cost was estimated by President José Sarney to be over US$100 million. It soon became apparent, however, that this was not simply a natural disaster; human action too had played a major part. For a number of years the wooded slopes of the surrounding mountains had been under increasing attack from the *favela* dwellers, who had cut down trees both for fuel and to clear a space on which to build their shacks. The combination of denuded hills and torrential rains resulted in the spate of water-borne rubbish which coursed through the *favelas*, bringing destruction in its wake.

Poor Brazilians do not choose to live in the squalor of the *favelas*; like poor people anywhere, they live in these conditions simply because they have little or no other option. Wages, for those fortunate enough to have work, are too low to enable them to live in the city proper, where rents are high. Yet the limited work opportunities that are available encourage people to migrate to the cities in ever-increasing numbers. This phenomenon, common throughout the underdeveloped countries of the South, is aggravated in Brazil's case by a high level of indebtedness. One result of this is that poor people are driven off land on which they supported themselves and their families, so that the land can instead be devoted to agricultural production for export. A "push" factor is thus added to the "pull" or attraction of urban areas for those searching for employment opportunities.

Third world cities are amongst the most rapidly growing areas in the world today. According to the report of the World Commission on Environment and Development (the so-called Brundtland Commission), in 1980 around 10% of the world's population lived in cities with populations of over 1 million; by the turn of the century the populations of urban centres in the Third World are expected to increase by an additional 750 million.[1]

◀ *The destruction of Amazonia: migrants drive through denuded forestland along the Vilhena-Colorado road. Rural unemployment in southern Brazil, exacerbated by the growth of cattle ranching and capital-intensive farming, has forced many to travel north or to the burgeoning cities.*

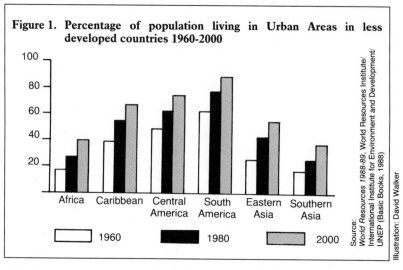

Figure 1. Percentage of population living in Urban Areas in less developed countries 1960-2000

Source: *World Resources 1988-89*, World Resources Institute/International Institute for Environment and Development/UNEP (Basic Books, 1988)

Illustration: David Walker

[ ] 1960   [■] 1980   [▨] 2000

Such a rate of increase can be attributed predominantly to the lack of economic opportunity available in rural areas and a belief — frequently encouraged by government policies — that the quality of life is better in urban areas.

The impact that people have on their environment is not limited to urban settlements. In Bangladesh during the latter part of 1987, and in northern India and again in Bangladesh in 1988, massive flooding of rice paddies and the countryside occurred. In addition to the loss of life, thousands of poor peasant farmers and their families lost their crops and homes, and the floods brought in their wake the threat of cholera, dysentry and other water-borne diseases. Here, too, many experts attributed the scale of the flooding to the denuding of the slopes of the Himalayas over a number of years, so that there is now no natural barrier to the spate of water running off the mountains.

A major reason for the increasing loss of forest cover is the dependence of the vast majority of the world's people on wood for basic domestic energy needs. According to the Brundtland Commission, some 2.5 billion (thousand million) people worldwide depend on fuelwood, crop residues and animal dung for this purpose.[2] Consumption on this scale would not be a cause for concern if sufficient reforestation were also taking place in the consuming countries. Regrettably, it is not. In all, according to the Commission, renewable energy resources provided 21% of all the energy consumed in the world — 15% in the form of biomass (wood, crop residues, animal dung etc) and 6% in the form of hydropower.

The loss of the world's forest cover is not solely due to the fuel needs of people in the Third World. Their hunger for land is equally compelling, and this may stem from many causes — for example, the unequal distribution of land in their societies, rapid increases in population, or the sheer need arising from acute poverty. Whatever the cause of such frontier expansion, it commonly has similar results. In Brazil's Amazon region, for example, an area ten times the size of Belgium is now cleared annually. Concern at the scale of this destruction led to the Brazilian government's announcement in September 1988 that it would no longer promote the colonisation of the region.

This is clearly good news, but environmentalists had expressed doubts about the desirability of the colonisation programme from its inception. The poor soil of the forest cannot sustain agriculture for long — about two to three years on average — and families then move on to clear new areas, leaving behind them desolate, denuded land. Similar problems are experienced in the Indonesian archipelago and in some African countries. Twenty million hectares of forest were destroyed in 1987 alone, some 8 million of them primary tropical forest; in 30 years' time, according to the Brundtland Commission, the area affected will be the size of India. At the same time, 6 million hectares a year of productive dryland, much of it in Africa, becomes worthless desert as a result of overuse and inappropriate cropping: the land lost in this way over 30 years will equal a desert the size of Saudi Arabia.

Yet poor people, understandably, do not concern themselves too much about environmental destruction when their day-to-day survival is at stake. Without money to invest in conservation measures such as terracing, the use of fertilisers, composting, crop rotation, water management and so on, and with so little land that they cannot afford to let it lie fallow, they have no choice but to continue using it until it is exhausted — thus placing their childrens' future in jeopardy.

It is this aspect which defines the *environmental* crisis facing the Third World as a *development* crisis. For, if poverty and the lack of access to sufficient resources to ensure at least a minimum level of life lie at the

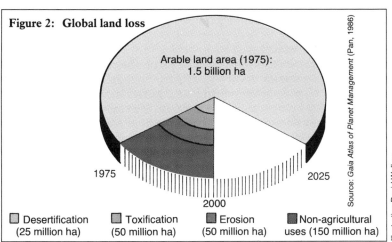

Figure 2: Global land loss

Arable land area (1975): 1.5 billion ha

1975

2000

2025

Source: Gaia Atlas of Planet Management (Pan, 1986)

Illustration:David Walker

▨ Desertification (25 million ha)   ▨ Toxification (50 million ha)   ▨ Erosion (50 million ha)   ■ Non-agricultural uses (150 million ha)

root of practices resulting in the environmental degradation taking place in so many third world countries, it is only by a concerted and successful effort to eradicate these causes that poor people will have the scope to demonstrate greater care for their environment.

Over the past four decades, attempts have been made to address the causes of poverty in third world countries. International institutions (such as the World Bank), the governments and the peoples of industrialised countries, and the governments of third world countries have joined forces, even if inadequately at times, in an effort to overcome the problems of third world poverty. This process, which has been called development, has had some notable successes: smallpox, for example, has been eradicated; more children survive and more people live longer, while recently-published research by a London-based development thinktank[3] has shown that average incomes in even the poorest countries have increased in real terms, albeit marginally.

This is obviously welcome news. But these achievements cannot hide the fact that, according to Barber Conable, president of the World Bank, 1 billion people in the Third World now live in extreme poverty (*Financial Times*, 28 September 1988), or that the gap between the quality of life in the industrialised world and the quality of life in the poorest third world countries has widened over the same period — and looks as if it will continue to grow wider still.

Most people in the industrialised world, and a growing number in the so-called middle-income countries of the Third World[4], eat better, use more energy and consume more natural resources than they did 40 years ago. Industrial production has increased fifty-fold since 1950, with 80% of this increase occurring in the industrialised countries. The consumption patterns of industrialised countries are grossly inequitable when compared with those of the majority of third world people; they also result in major problems of pollution, not only for the developed countries but for third world countries too.

Waste disposal or dumping?
With the increasing sophistication of industrial processes, disposal of the consumer societies' waste, be it ordinary household garbage or the dangerous by-products of industry such as nuclear waste or poisonous chemicals, has become a serious problem. One aspect of that problem was graphically illustrated in 1987 when some of New York's household rubbish was towed to the Caribbean and back in an effort to find somewhere to dispose of it. A popular song, "The Garbage Barge", rose to the top of the US music charts, but the incident also emphasised that the consumer society is now producing more rubbish than it can hope to cope with safely.

Nor is the US alone in this. European countries, including Britain, also experience problems of waste disposal. Recent efforts of the environmentalist movement, Greenpeace, to prevent the dumping and burning of waste at sea have attracted media attention and the unfavourable publicity may underlie the reported interest of European companies in finding sites for industrial and nuclear waste disposal in third world countries.[5] So seriously did some African governments take these approaches that the issue was discussed in the Organisation of African Unity (OAU), which concluded that the continent should not be used as a European rubbish tip.

In the eyes of some African governments the chance of earning additional foreign exchange appeared, regrettably, to be more important than the possible health implications for their populations. The government of the West African state of Benin has reportedly signed an agreement with the Gibraltar-based firm, Sesco, for the dumping of between 1 and 5 million tonnes of industrial waste over the next decade, for which it is alleged to have received US$3 a tonne. Despite the government's denial, there have been unconfirmed reports that two shiploads of French waste were recently dumped in the country. In February 1988 it was reported from Strasbourg that several European companies had signed a US$120 million-a-year contract with Guinea-Bissau for the import of 3 million tonnes of industrial waste each year.

Governments may not even be aware that waste is being dumped in their countries. In mid-1988 the Nigerian government protested to Italy following investigations which revealed that a Nigerian citizen had been paid US$1,000 a month to store drums of Italian toxic waste. The government, which had taken a strong line at the OAU against African countries accepting industrial waste from Europe, only became aware of the waste's presence in Nigeria because of the activities of Nigerian students in Italy. The students drew the Nigerian government's attention to Italian press reports that the shipments had started in September 1987. Both Britain and the United States sent experts to Nigeria to advise the government on the most appropriate way to deal with the waste. They reported that the 8,000-10,000 drums of waste, which had been dumped about a mile from the Nigerian port of Koko, were "extremely dangerous".

According to Mark Line, an environmental scientist, and Dr Barry Lambert, a radiation specialist, the drums contained acidic wastes, chlorinated hydro-carbons, waste paints and unidentified semi-solid materials. As many as half of them were "in an appalling physical condition [with] an immediate risk of fire or explosion". Removal of the waste was reported to require "elaborate equipment and a large team of qualified personnel" at an estimated cost of over £1 million. The Nigerian government, while welcoming the offer of expert assistance and the absence of any radioactive materials in the waste, demanded that Italy should repatriate its waste and seized two Italian-owned ships, the second of which was seemingly carrying yet more waste bound for Nigeria.

Towards the end of June 1988 this pressure appeared to have worked.

The four Italian companies from which the waste had originated offered to remove it. However, the scientists' report indicated that this would be a lengthy and complicated exercise, possibly fraught with danger as there was a risk that any movement of the material could set off an explosion, allowing the wind to carry poisonous smoke over a large area. In the event, the waste was finally loaded on a ship, the *Karin B*, and left Nigeria. But it was not until late September 1988 that the final destination of the *Karin B*'s cargo was decided. Having unsuccessfully

Scientists in protective clothing examine containers of Italian toxic waste dumped near the Nigerian port of Koko.

attempted to dock in Britain and France, the *Karin B* was ordered by the cargo's owners to head for Italy where the cargo was off-loaded, despite vociferous opposition from residents of the area surrounding the port of Livorno.

Such dumping of toxic waste in third world countries is a flagrant breach of a European Commission directive. The failure of all but two of the member states to enshrine the European Commission's directive in domestic law is a harsh reminder of the lack of practical concern in this area. The Commission announced at the end of June 1988 that it would be taking action to ensure compliance. This is clearly to be welcomed, as was the British government's decision in September to incorporate the directive in British law. However, one is forced to ask whether any attention would have been paid to the matter had it not been for the actions of the Nigerian students in Italy.

African countries are not the only ones in the Third World to have displayed an interest in earning foreign exchange by accepting industrial and nuclear waste. The *Financial Times* of 8 June 1988 reported that the government of Argentina was seriously considering accepting nuclear waste for disposal, despite the huge risks involved.

14

Atmospheric pollution

On a global scale, humanity's impact on the environment appears alarming. According to scientific reports — some of which date back at least 15 years — the ozone layer of the earth's atmosphere, which absorbs the sun's harmful ultraviolet rays, is under attack. Scientists have discovered "holes" in the ozone layer above both the Arctic and the Antarctic, as well as significant thinning over Siberia, and it is generally accepted that this has been caused by man-made air pollutants, including chlorofluorocarbon (CFC) gas used in refrigerators, as a propellant in many spray aerosols and in the manufacture of polystyrene packaging. Should this destruction continue, the risk to people's health is predicted to be of frightening proportions. Research by US scientists suggests that for every 1% decrease of ozone in the stratosphere (the layer between the earth's atmosphere and space), the incidence of skin cancers will rise by between 2% and 3%.

The level of carbon dioxide in the earth's atmosphere has increased significantly since the advent of the industrial revolution, which was accompanied by a dramatic increase in the use of fossil fuels; and the process is believed to have speeded up considerably with the increasing deforestation of recent years. Scientists believe that this could have major effects on the earth's climate, possibly raising the temperature by as much as between 2°C and 3°C, as heat which would previously have been reflected off the earth's surface and back into space is now trapped by the carbon dioxide and unable to escape.

This "greenhouse" effect has serious potential consequences. Scientists calculate that an increase of as little as one degree centigrade in the average temperature would result in massive crop losses in the grain-producing areas of North America and Central Asia. On the other hand, the world's rice growing areas might benefit but the temporary disruption would be great. Melting polar ice would add to this disruption, raising the sea level by up to 6 metres and devastating low-lying coastal regions.[6] Other types of air pollution are caused by the emission of smoke with a high sulphur content, particularly from coal-fired power stations. Scientists have directly linked these emissions to acid rain, which has destroyed European forests both on the Continent and in Scotland, as well as sterilising inland lakes.

International concern over the extent of such pollution poses major challenges to third world countries wishing to industrialise. They are caught in the cleft stick of either having to accept increased costs to avoid existing sources of pollution or to search for alternative sources of power, which may themselves prove ultimately to be equally damaging to the environment.

Water pollution

Mankind is producing more and more pollution too, not all, nor possibly even the greater part, of which is in solid form. The pumping of sewage sludge into the North Sea has been linked to the sudden expansion of algae-growth off the Scandanavian coast during 1988; the deoxygenating effects of its death killed off sea life in these coastal areas. And sewage sludge is suspected by some scientists to be a possible cause of the development of a diphtheria-related virus which is devastating the European common seal population. Fishermen have long blamed both increasing pollution and over-fishing for the decline of the European fishing industry: reduced catches and lower quality fish are now an everyday reality.

The world's seas are not the only repository of mankind's pollutants. Inland waterways, too, are becoming increasingly polluted: some scientists believe that in industralised countries, including Britain, poisons from landfill sites where rubbish is dumped have leached into the watertable, threatening the purity of the water supply. Industrial accidents — like that which occurred in 1986, when chemicals accidently released into the Rhine in Switzerland poisoned the river as far as its mouth in Holland — have added to such pollution. Far more serious in its effects has been the failure to enforce adequate industrial pollution controls, particularly in third world countries, where, in their desire to keep costs down and maximise profits, industries are content with standards which would be unacceptable in the First World. The increasing industrialisation of modern agriculture has also been a significant cause of fresh-water pollution. Biocides (fungicides, herbicides and pesticides) and fertilisers have leached into rivers and lakes, poisoning aquatic life and ultimately deoxygenating the water, making it incapable of sustaining life.

Land degradation
Industrial agricultural practices have also contributed to a decline in the fertility of the land. This is not a particularly recent phenomenon — John Steinbeck's novel, *The Grapes of Wrath*, painted a graphic picture of the cumulative effects of inappropriate farming methods in the US mid-west during the 1930s — but the spread of single cropping, which gives the land no chance to recover from one harvest to the next, and the dramatic increase in the size of farms has speeded up the process alarmingly. If modern agricultural methods have had a damaging effect on the heavier soils of the world's temperate zones — it has been estimated, for example, that without massive applications of fertiliser much of Britain's farmland will become unable to support crops within the next 20 years — they are even less appropriate to the fragile soils of the tropics. Cutting and burning the forest cover will give a one-off fillip to the fertility of such soil, but intensive cropping quickly exhausts the land, leaving it barren. The pattern is the same in those parts of the world where inappropriate farming practices go hand-in-hand with widespread deforestation. In such places the deserts are advancing; and as people move on in search of new land on which to plant their crops or graze their animals, the process merely speeds up.

Photo: David Hoffman

Deforestation and the ensuing land degradation can have disastrous results: in January 1989 the village of Ban Huay Ko, Thailand, was destroyed by floods resulting from overlogging.

Something, it seems, has become seriously dislocated in the world's development process. The coexistence of conspicuous over-consumption in the First World and unacceptable under-consumption throughout the Third World must raise questions about the development process to date. How is it possible that the efforts of the past four decades have resulted in the present situation, which sees more hungry people in the world than ever before, more people who are illiterate, without access to safe water or adequate shelter, and who live in a world where environmental destruction threatens the future security of all? Can this process really be described as "development"?

Any attempt to address these questions has to return to fundamental issues. To do this, it is necessary to examine what development has meant in practice and how the theories of development have supported its practical application. Space alone makes it impossible to review every development project which has been implemented since 1950. What is needed is to identify the main assumptions underpinning the models used by the major participants in the development process and to put these alongside a number of representative practical examples. The following chapters, therefore, will outline the origins of the theory and practice of development. The attempt will then be made to illustrate the practical results. To use the analogy of an umbrella, the early chapters seek to observe the theory and practice of development over the past 40 years from above, viewing the exterior of the development umbrella. In later chapters, we will go under the umbrella to examine development from the perspective of the poor, who experience the process directly.

Briefly, we will attempt to show that, by focusing only on the economic aspect of the human condition, development theory over the past four decades has been conceptually limited and that, as a result and in spite of the gains that have been made, conventional practice has failed to achieve development in the fullest sense of the word — that is, the sustainable realisation by all peoples of their full human potential.

Notes

1. *Our Common Future: Report of the World Commission on Environment and Development*, Oxford University Press (Oxford, 1987).

2. The extent to which people depend on wood to meet their fuel needs is clear from a 1983 study by the UN Food and Agricultural Organisation (FAO). This showed that 1.3 billion people were solely dependent on wood for fuel and were consuming it faster than it was being grown. Of the 95 countries covered by the study, 21, mostly in Africa, relied on wood for 75% of their energy needs. Fuelwood was an important source of energy in all the countries studied.

3. *The Rich and the Poor: Changes in Incomes of Developing Countries since 1960*, Overseas Development Institute Briefing Paper (London, June 1988).

4. Defined by the World Bank as those countries whose per capita GNP is between US$460 and US$7,410 per annum. *World Development Report, 1988*, Oxford University Press (Oxford, 1988).

5. See the *Observer*, 29 May and 5 June 1988, for reports of approaches to African countries.

6. Much of London, for example, would be flooded were this to occur. Far more serious, however, would be the expected flooding of about 20% of Bangladesh and at least six Indian and Pacific Ocean island states, including the Maldive Islands, which would be one of the first countries to disappear beneath the rising ocean level.

CHAPTER 2

FORTY YEARS OF DEVELOPMENT THEORY AND PRACTICE

The last 40 years have been dominated by two distinct strands of development theory. For roughly the first 15, what was known as "modernisation theory" prevailed, while latterly development has been underpinned by "integration theory"[7] — though as Richard Higgott points out in *Political Development Theory* (1983), what changed was not so much the basic assumptions as the mood surrounding the practitioners of development. Whereas the initial phase, loosely connected with the first United Nations Development Decade in the 1960s, was characterised by a spirit of optimism, the latter period, equally loosely associated with the third UN Development Decade in the 1980s, has been marked by pessimism. In between came a period of growing doubt about the validity of past certainties, which manifested itself in an increased questioning of the theory and, even more obviously, in the actual practice of those most closely involved in development during the 1970s — in particular the World Bank under the presidency of Robert McNamara.

Cubatao, in Brazil, is one of the most polluted industrial centres on earth; its air contains twice the level of industrial particles considered dangerous by the World Health Organisation. Is this the goal towards which traditional development theory has been working?

Photo: Sebastio Salgado/Panos Pictures

Modernisation theory

Based largely on work done between 1945 and 1963 by the US Social Sciences Research Council's Committee on Comparative Politics, under the chairmanship of Gabriel Almond, modernisation theory reflected the optimism of the post-war world. The prevailing belief in US circles was that the development and continued growth of a scientific social science would form the basis for successful social engineering in both the First and the Third Worlds. And despite the occasional signs that things might not be so rosy, such was the experience of the First World

A Tigrayan woman with an earthenware water-carrier. Many millions of people in the developing world still lack access to adequate water supplies; fetching water can involve an arduous trek, often lasting several hours.

Photo: Mike Goldwater/NETWORK

that this belief was questioned less than might otherwise have been the case. By the mid-1950s, not only had the Western democracies triumphed over fascism, but Marxism too had largely fallen into disrepute due to the exposure of Stalinist oppression in the Soviet Union. In the industrialised world absolute poverty seemed to be a thing of the past and people believed that, with increasing prosperity, relative poverty too would cease to be a source of social tension. Unemployment stood at historically low levels, while guaranteed access to education and the availability of welfare benefits were seen to be reducing acknowledged social inequalities. Any problems which remained appeared capable of resolution through the technological advances which Western societies would inevitably make.

It is against this background that the contribution made to the elaboration of development theory by social scientists such as Almond, Talcott Parsons and David Easton, along with economists such as Walt Rostow, must be judged. Fundamental to the theory which they collectively advanced is an acceptance of Western industrialised democracy as the ultimate goal for all societies, particularly those in the Third World.

Put simply, modernisation theory sought to reproduce Western democratic industrialised society in the developing world. It set out to achieve an increase in third world countries' wealth by maximising economic growth — and industrialisation (including the industrialisation of agriculture) was believed to be the most efficient way of achieving such increased growth levels — the benefits of which, it was believed, would "trickle down" to the poor over time through greater employment opportunities. For these theorists, modern society equalled industrialised society and the transformation to industrialised society was regarded as a desirable aim. Little attention was paid to already existing patterns of social and cultural order. Such attention as was given to them was always from the perspective that these traditional structures were impediments to economic growth — which, it must be admitted, they often were. However, the scale of the task which the development theorists set themselves and their confidence in the overwhelming rightness of their beliefs brooked no impediment. Traditionalism and traditional practices were anti-progress; even worse, they were dysfunctional to the grand plan to reproduce Western-style democracies throughout the world.

One should not attribute perverse motives to these individuals. If they saw traditional patterns of behaviour as rooted in the essentially conservative nature of a peasant-based social order and as negative influences on change, it was because they believed that only by following Western democratic models could the people of the Third World hope to improve their lot. Only by modernising their economies would they be able to guarantee that the benefits of increased production and the accompanying increase in wealth would trickle down to the poor. After all, they reasoned, if absolute poverty was now a thing of the past in the industrialised world, similar development strategies would also result in its disappearance from the Third World.

Modernisation theorists accepted that social tensions might well result from this policy. However, they firmly believed that not only were the problems of economic modernisation capable of resolution through technical means, but so too was any social conflict arising from these economic changes. With the benefit of hindsight it is clear that the theory failed to take into account the power which traditional structures could mobilise in their defence. Thus, rather than increasing the wealth of society as a whole, and even where a government sympathetic to promoting the interests of the majority of the population existed, the development programmes implemented often resulted in massive increases of wealth for third world elites and few, if any, real benefit for the poor. Traditional elites frequently formed political alliances with members of the modern sector of the economy (eg industry, business, and export agriculture) to ensure the continuation of their privileges.

Classically, development programmes during this period were what came to be known as "pharaonic". They included massive expenditure on irrigation, infrastructure, and industrialisation. Little attention was paid to promoting agricultural development, except in the commercial sector producing for the export market and thereby helping provide the additional foreign exchange needed for ongoing investment in the industrial and plantation-based agricultural sectors. Domestic agricultural production, after all, was viewed as the preserve of the traditionalists, the most conservative of whom were seen to be the peasantry.

In the early stages of the development process, before an economy reached the famous "take-off point" postulated in Walt Rostow's economic theory (after which self-sustaining economic growth would be achieved), the shortage of investment capital in third world countries meant that they had to borrow or encourage foreign investment. But in order to service the foreign debt they had to export more and more. Thus, increasing emphasis came to be placed on production for the export market in both the traditional (principally smallholding agriculture) and modern sectors of the economy.

Development projects implemented during this period actively promoted this focus. Infrastructural projects were designed to increase the outward focus of third world economies. In Ghana, for example, the construction of a dam, financed by the World Bank and the British government amongst others, was conceived as having a twofold purpose. The stored water would be used to irrigate farmland growing export crops, while the hydro-electricity generated was to be used to smelt bauxite for sale on the international market as aluminium. Any power left would be used in the capital, Accra.

The Akosombo dam on the River Volta was completed in 1966, the year that President Kwame Nkrumah was overthrown in a military coup. The waters behind the dam wall cover an area of 8,482 square kilometres, more than three times the size of Luxembourg. One per cent of Ghana's population (78,000 people) from 700 towns and villages was uprooted by the dam. But, 20 years after its completion, the basis for its construction — a contract between the Kaiser Aluminium Company and the Ghanaian government — no longer exists; Kaiser does not use Ghanaian bauxite now, importing it instead from Jamaica for processing into alumina in Ghana before re-exporting to the United States for refining into aluminium. Nor have any of the expected secondary benefits (accelerated industrialisation, improved transport to the interior along the 300-kilometre-long lake, and a general spreading of development through an improvement in the quality of life enjoyed by Ghanaians) been realised. Thus the dam's sole benefit to Ghana has been the location of an alumina processing plant in the country, which is supplied with electricity at uneconomic rates based on the contract with Kaiser Aluminium.

There was clearly little direct benefit envisaged for poor Ghanaians from this project. But the prevailing fundamental belief that if one increased the wealth of some people in a country, at least part of that wealth would trickle down to the poorest, meant that targeting aid at the poorest was unnecessary. In the event, such trickle-down rarely occurred; and when it did, it resulted only in ensuring that poor people were no worse off than before, while the elites grew considerably richer.

Nonetheless, the achievements of this phase (the 1960s) should not be altogether discounted. Investment on the scale which occurred during this period inevitably resulted in some improvements for ordinary people, such as improved access to health care, increased educational provision, improved links between some rural areas and the major producing centres and increased, even if still inadequate, employment opportunities.

However, this strategy of promoting economic growth resulted in an ever-widening gap between the fortunes of urban and rural areas. It was obviously desirable, from a potential investor's point of view, to site any investment as close as possible to the infrastructure which already existed. Cost factors alone — the need to ensure supplies of electricity and access to roads and rail — dictated this. Such domestic investment as occurred tended to go to the newly-independent countries' urban areas, or areas already well served by existing communications. Furthermore, potential investors required a workforce with a certain level of skills and this was more likely to be found in urban than rural areas.

The effect of these perfectly rational preferences on the part of investors was not limited to aggravating urban-rural inequality: improved employment prospects, however limited, encouraged migration to the urban areas, and the growing urban populations placed greater strains on already inadequate basic services — such as public health and housing — which necessitated still greater urban investment.

Thus, the application of modernisation theory encouraged both the speeding up of urbanisation and the concentration of investment in third world towns and cities.

Very often such concentration of investment was also encouraged by third world governments for political reasons. Closer, both geographically and politically, to urban than to rural populations, the newly-independent governments were often more concerned to meet the needs and aspirations of urban residents than their rural counterparts. Emphasis in health care was placed on cure rather than prevention and there was substantially greater investment in urban hospitals than in rural health-posts. Similarly, as agriculture was viewed largely as a means to increase export revenue in order to help finance the economy's modernisation and the growth of an industrial base, agricultural policy *per se* was neglected in many countries. In far too many cases this meant that governments and expert advisers took a short-term view of the contribution which agriculture could make to the development of a country as a whole — as the unrealistically low prices offered to agricultural producers show.

Worst affected by this neglect were farmers producing food for domestic consumption. Crop prices were kept unprofitably low because of the government's desire to hold down urban food prices. Such extension services (government agricultural advice/training schemes) as were available were targeted at those producing export crops, leaving most food producers without advice on improved farming methods. Those who did benefit from extension advice and technological advances — through the Green Revolution package as in Indonesia and the Punjab (see Chapter 3) — were usually wealthier, able to afford the financial costs of the package, and identified by the donor community as being the most modern in their approach.

Thus, while there were undoubted achievements in following modernisation theory, they were sufficient neither in scale nor in widespread distribution to maintain the optimism first displayed by the theorists. Doubt and pessimism began to be voiced concerning the correctness of the strategy while the timescale necessary for eradicating poverty was clearly seen to be far longer than had previously been anticipated. Theorists then began to look at the internal political constraints operating against the achievement of Western-style industrial democracies in the Third World. The body of thinking which subsequently developed became known as "integration theory".

Integration theory

Two important features of integration theory are worth commenting upon at the outset. Firstly, the extent to which it ignored all academic thinking other than that epitomised by modernisation theory. There is no indication, for example, that integrationists believed it necessary to take into account either earlier Marxist theories or the "dependency" theorists who emerged from the work of the UN Economic Commission for Latin America during the 1950s and 1960s, and who made a far broader analysis of the poverty endemic in Latin America and the Third World generally. Secondly, the integrationists attempted to ensure that economic theory was inextricably woven into the domestic political process (hence their name). Whereas their forerunners (the modernisationists) had apparently believed that if one got the economic process of development right the political process, including democratisation, would follow, the integrationists stressed the importance of welding the two from the beginning.

Thus, integration theory focused on the domestic political economy of third world countries, and ignored the way in which the international market often worked to the detriment of third world countries; and it stressed the importance of addressing what it saw as the vital political question of internal resource allocation — which groups of people received which resources. The principal reason for this latter concern was the obvious failure of modernisation theory to meet the aspirations of the poorer strata in third world societies for an improved quality of life for themselves and their families.

Despite these differences, what stands out most clearly is the great similarity between the two theories. Integration theory laid less stress than its predecessor on the modern sector, but both regarded its expansion as the key to success. For example, economic growth was re-emphasised as both a desirable and a necessary goal for countries wanting to develop, and Walt Rostow remained the guiding beacon. Economic growth was also necessary if the political goals of the analysts

Illustration: Ted Trainer/Green Print

were to be achieved. These aims were not fundamentally different from those at the root of modernisation theory — namely, the emergence of societies modelled on Western industrialised democracies. The integrationists further refined the process which developing countries would have to go through. They saw a sixfold task for third world leaders: to ensure national survival; establish a national identity; integrate the society; create an acceptable system of authority; mobilise and distribute resources; and secure freedom from external control.

These six goals all seem desirable, particularly when one remembers that many third world countries achieved national independence only during the 1960s and that their populations often comprise people of differing ethnic, cultural, linguistic and religious backgrounds. Those tasks which may be most important for our purposes here are the third and the final two listed — that is integrating the society, mobilising and distributing resources and securing freedom from external control. What the integrationists failed to ask, however, was: what type of integration is required; which resources should be distributed, from where and to whom; and freedom from what type of external control?

Failure to address these questions meant that the practice emerging from the theoretical structure differed little from that of earlier modernisation theory. Unshakeable belief in the value of economic growth, trickle-down and the importance of production for the export market, which regrettably tends to downgrade the value of production for domestic consumption, remain as much at the heart of development as practised under integration theory as they were under modernisation theory. The failure to address the three crucial questions led to an emphasis on domestic policy, almost to the point of excluding any external influences, and to a neglect of the consequences of increasing commodity production for foreign-exchange earnings, which often meant that the careful calculations of the theorists were thrown awry within very short periods.

During the 1970s, under Robert McNamara's presidency of the World Bank, there was a shift of emphasis in the Bank's development policy towards funding agricultural projects. This was welcomed by donors and recipients alike, particularly in view of the Bank's stated intention of emphasising projects which would benefit the poorer sections of third world societies — the so-called "basic needs approach". The practice, however, proved to be very different from the rhetoric, as can be seen in the example of the World Bank-funded SIS project described in Case Study 1 (see p.31). The underlying principles remained the same: projects were still large-scale, capital-intensive, and orientated towards production for export rather than domestic consumption.

In many instances there was no difference in the type of project funded. Dams, for example, continued to be built at considerable expense; what was now emphasised in the speeches and literature was the potential agricultural benefits accruing from the dam through

GOT ANY CHANGE TO SPARE MR ARAB? I'D RATHER NOT GET INVOLVED!

'... SO YOU SEE, THE ENTIRE FUTURE OF THE INTERNATIONAL FINANCIAL SYSTEM HINGES ON YOUR CAPACITY FOR QUICK RECOVERY AND VAST ECONOMIC GROWTH.'

Illustration: Oliphant

irrigation, rather than the generation of power. Infrastructural projects to improve communications continued to be funded without any significant changes in design. Their purpose remained the same: to enable the transport of goods for export to the world market. And, as is shown by Case Study 2 (see p.34), national efforts to increase the availability of foreign exchange also remained in the same tradition.

In any event, the McNamara period was limited in its impact. By the latter part of the 1970s, donor governments, led by the World Bank, had begun to stress policy reforms to an even greater extent than policy design, particularly with regard to Latin American and sub-Saharan African countries, where the impact of the debt crisis in the 1980s was most severe. There was a shift away from narrow and focused "project aid" towards broader "programme" and "sector aid". Programmes were designed to increase production still further so that the accumulated debts could be serviced, and third world economies opened up further to imports.

The theoretical process from economic stabilisation through structural adjustment to recovery, which characterised the 1980s, represented the pinnacle of the integrationists' achievements, provided that one accepts the limited definitions of the tasks facing third world political leaders and the lack of any active role in the process for third world peoples. It also remained directly in the modernisation tradition. Current policy underscores earlier beliefs in the need to modernise third world economies and, although there is no longer a necessary emphasis on urban industrialisation, this remains a feature where donors are convinced that a country has a comparative advantage.

In essence, therefore, there has been little substantive change in the theoretical foundations of development, other than a more explicit recognition of the need to integrate domestic economic and political decisions. Fundamental to the process, in the view of the practitioners, is the need to promote economic growth through increased production of goods and commodities for sale on the international market. The foreign exchange thus earned is to be used for debt service, with any surplus to be invested in further development (see Case Study 2).

As in the past, it is recognised that third world countries are unlikely to be able to find all the necessary capital resources for this process. They are still encouraged to borrow the balance, although it is accepted that under present circumstances this may be very difficult for some countries. Currently, a far greater role is envisaged for foreign private investment as a source of the necessary additional capital, but those countries which have implemented economic recovery programmes along the lines recommended by the World Bank and other aid donors commonly find it easier to borrow on the international market.

The design of economic recovery or structural adjustment programmes continues in the tradition of integration theory. Necessary internal economic reforms are stressed — for example, the prices paid to agricultural producers, or the extent of state involvement in the economy — and little attention is paid to the external economic climate. While it is true that the World Bank itself has no expertise to deal with

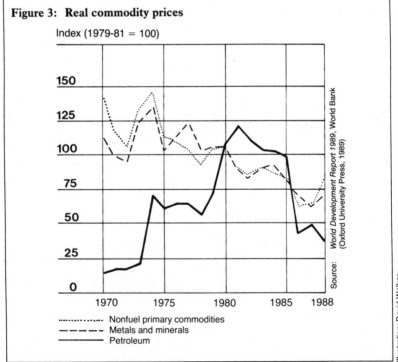

Figure 3: Real commodity prices

Index (1979-81 = 100)

Source: *World Development Report 1989*, World Bank (Oxford University Press, 1989)

Illustration: David Walker

·············· Nonfuel primary commodities
— — — — Metals and minerals
———— Petroleum

such matters, its increasingly close co-operation with the International Monetary Fund (IMF) and the role which the major Western industrial economies play in the determination of IMF policy suggest that the recommended domestic reforms could be far better matched to their likely international economic effects.

Regrettably, this seldom occurs. Thus commodity producers are encouraged to increase production for sale in the international market, with little concern for the likely impact this will have on commodity prices. Where attempts have been made at forward commodity price projection, by the IMF and World Bank amongst others, these have often proved hopelessly inadequate. Prices have frequently fallen when they were expected to remain stable or even to rise somewhat, or have fallen far more sharply than predicted due, in part at least, to the increased supply available in a declining market where technological advances in industrialised countries have replaced natural commodities with synthetic products.

In an ongoing effort to earn the foreign exchange envisaged under the economic recovery programmes, governments have encouraged still further production, forcing the unit price of commodities down even more. The collapse of commodity prices, and of the prices of other goods produced in third world countries, has wreaked havoc with the earnings projections in the agreed economic recovery programmes, and this has severely undermined the ability of countries to import their fundamental requirements. And while there have been recoveries in the prices of some commodities during 1987 and 1988, many third world producers have failed to reap the full benefit of these, owing to, amongst other things, a serious shortage of spare parts needed to maximise production.

Increasingly, third world countries are running faster and faster in a desperate, and frequently hopeless, attempt to protect the small gains they have been able to achieve. For many countries, particularly on the African continent, the progress achieved in the 1970s, as measured by social indicators like the infant mortality rate, access to health care and primary education, etc, is now being reversed. In some countries these indices have now returned to their level at independence, while for others there has been no improvement throughout the 1980s. Taking population growth into account, they have been able to achieve at best no more than a maintenance of already inadequate standards for their people throughout the 1980s.

The cost of such regression and standstill has been huge. In many instances, the ever-increasing requirement to produce more for export has placed impossible burdens on a fragile environment. The most productive land has increasingly been given over to export production, forcing food producers onto more marginal land. In its turn, this has resulted in some areas in nomadic herders being forced to use land for grazing which cannot sustain their herds. This process has resulted in the further impoverishment of both groups and made them more vulnerable to harsh weather conditions and the disruption and destruction resulting from conflict (see Chapter 5 for further discussion of these points).

This was certainly not the outcome expected by the development planners and practitioners, who believed that the implementation of development programmes would necessarily lead to a continuing improvement in the living conditions of third world people. In pursuing policies aimed at increasing economic growth, they ignored the warnings of individuals like Barbara Ward and René Dubois (*Only One Earth: The Care and Maintenance of A Small Planet*, 1972) who argued that the costs resulting from "driving blindly for economic growth" without considering the social and environmental implications were "potentially catastrophic". By measuring development exclusively in standard economic terms, such as using gross national product per capita as an indicator of economic growth, conventional theory ignored the underlying purpose of the process.

For CAFOD and many other non-governmental organisations (NGOs) involved in development, as well as for numerous individuals both in government and in the multilateral aid organisations themselves, the question is the same as it was in the 1970s: how have the policies which were followed affected the quality of life of the poorest 40% of the people? For although an increase in the disposable income of third world people forms one part of development it cannot of itself guarantee full human development. It is at least as important to allow people to free themselves from the constraints which both cause their poverty and perpetuate it. In other words, if development is to occur, it should promote the conditions which allow them to realise their full human potential, thereby guaranteeing their sustained progress in the future.

To this end, NGOs have repeatedly emphasised the need to respect local experience and expertise, and involve the community in the planning, implementation and evaluation of development projects. There are two two main reasons for this. Firstly, experience has shown that greater community involvement improves the chances of success; and secondly, by drawing widely on the various skills that exist within a community, this approach can build up people's confidence in dealing with other day to day problems which they face. Although economic growth clearly has a part to play in the development process, an increased national income will not, of itself, guarantee development for the poor — indeed it may even retard the process. It is important, therefore, to examine some examples of projects and programmes funded by the major donors to see in greater detail the extent to which they were in line with the theoretical underpinning of development.

Notes

7. "Public policy analysis" is the precise term, although "integration theory" is used more often because it indicates the contents more clearly.

CASE STUDY ONE
TRIBAL PEOPLES IN INDIA RESIST WORLD BANK FINANCED IRRIGATION PROGRAMME

Indian villagers drawing water from a pond. Irrigation schemes often ignore traditional methods and result in local people losing their ancient homelands and sometimes their livelihood.

In the late 1970s the World Bank agreed to provide US$127 million for the development of an integrated irrigation and agricultural project in the Singhbum district of the Indian state of Bihar. This project is essentially similar to previous development projects, such as the Ghanaian dam discussed earlier (see pp.22-23). The Bank's feasibility study expressed the belief that "if development of the Suvernarekha Irrigation System (SIS) does not take place, water scarcity would be the single most important constraint to agro-economic growth, especially in the Bihar part of the project area". As envisaged, the SIS will consist of two dams, one at Chandil on the River Suvernarekha, with a reservoir capacity of 1,963 million cubic metres, and the other at Icha on the Kharkai river, with a reservoir capacity of 1,043 million cubic metres.

The dams and the diversion of the River Suvernarekha mean that the original users — chiefly the Santhals, the Ho, the Bhumij, the Gond and the Munda — have to move to new land or are denied the use of the river. These people have vigorously opposed the project, and continue to do so. In 1978, during a peaceful hunger-strike to demonstrate this opposition, the state police opened fire and killed Ghanshyam Mahto, one of the leaders of the protest movement, and seven villagers. Now organised under the Visthapit Mukti Vahini (Liberation for the Displaced) movement launched at the time, the protest against the dam continues. During 1987, for example, two massive processions were organised by Visthapit Mukti Vahini on 3 September and again over 18-23 December.

Popular opposition to the Icha dam is, if anything, even stronger. During 1982, one of the protest's leaders, ex-serviceman Ganga Ram Kalundia, was brutally murdered. The Delhi-based Commissioner for Scheduled Tribes and Castes, Ms Sunil Basant, in a recent report on popular opposition to the SIS, confirmed police responsiblty for Kalundia's murder and recommended that the SIS should be shelved. Opposition to the dam is organised by Jharkhand Mukti Andolan, and supporters have pledged non-violent resistance to the construction because it threatens to uproot them culturally, socially and economically.

In the World Bank's view, it is totally irrational for people who live in an area of water shortage to oppose a plan which would provide them with the water they need to improve their standard of living. However, there are two very good reasons for their opposition. Firstly, the area and those who live there are not starved of water. Secondly, the dams, rather than bringing them economic and social improvement, will deprive them of their ancient homelands.

Reports from the SIS area state that all the villages already have irrigation facilities. In this hilly region, run-off rainwater is collected in storage tanks, constructed by forming an embankment along the slopes. Below the surface, layers of granite and gneiss form an impermeable layer of rock which reduces water loss through seepage. Such tanks are clearly appropriate to the region. The villagers farm rice in low-lying fields irrigated from the tanks above them. This method of farming is so successful that more than one crop of rice and wheat is harvested annually. Upland varieties of rice, which are also grown by the villagers, are entirely rain-fed and do not require irrigation. These are grown in rotation with wheat, mung, mustard, gram, surgujia, dhania, and other traditional crops to maintain the soil's fertility and provide a diversity of crops for local consumption and sale.

The World Bank's assessment of the project's feasibility ignored the ingenuity of the tribal people and the genetic diversity of their food base, which provides a high physical quality of life. Instead, it argued that the local people had "been slow in adopting modern technologies, and their standard of living has been generally lower than that of the rest of the population". This is undoubtedly true when measured by the standard of disposable cash income but such a measure fails to take into account the true total wealth of tribal economies, derived, in no small part, directly from the wealth of nature.

The Bank's motives in supporting the project financially are sincere. Using their limited measure of wealth, the assessment team calculated that 80% of the people in the area were below the poverty line and that the project would reduce this to 25%. The means by which this will be achieved are to induce these people to abandon their traditional — and proven — methods of farming in favour of single crops, grown from hybrid seeds which require fertilisers, biocides and large quantities of irrigation. The seed, fertiliser and biocides have to be bought.

Leaving on one side the experience of indebtedness, pollution and ecological vulnerability which have resulted from the adoption of such farming practices elsewhere, there are sound reasons to doubt the validity of the system proposed. Because of the type of rock below the surface of the soil, the intensive irrigation required by hybrid seeds will result in waterlogging of the most fertile pockets of low-lying land. A far sounder irrigation system would be to add to the existing network of tanks improving these where necessary. However, such a system would fail to supply the extra water needed for further industrial expansion in Jamshedpur, the most important industrial centre in the area, whereas under the SIS the city would be supplied with 727 million cubic metres of water, 654 million from the Chandil dam and 73 million from the Icha. Thus, the dams are being constructed essentially to supply water for municipal and private industrial use; but in order to justify the project, and particularly the fact that US$55 million of the total World Bank loan will be spent outside India buying equipment and expertise on the international market, emphasis was placed on assistance to a group of people who neither need nor want development of this type.

Dr Vandana Shiva, co-ordinator of the Indian-based Research Foundation for Science, Technology and Natural Resource Policy, believes that projects such as the SIS raise a number of important and basic questions about development aid. Why, she asks, should ordinary Indians bear the interest burden of a loan, the beneficiaries of which are private industry in India and abroad? She also questions why Western tax-payers should be taxed to provide aid funds, the result of which is to make third world elites, and their own already rich countries, even richer. But, most importantly, she asks why tribal peoples and their customs should be sacrificed to suit large-scale private industry.

Source: Third World Network Features, Penang, Malaysia.

CASE STUDY TWO
INDIGENOUS PEOPLE IN SARAWAK, BORNEO, UNITE TO RESIST LOGGING IN THE WORLD'S OLDEST RAINFOREST

Photo: Nigel Dickinson

Penan tribesmen blockading forest roads in order to disrupt the activities of the timber companies.

The exports of hardwood logs is an increasingly important source of foreign-exchange earnings for third world countries short of much-needed hard currency. Malaysia is no exception to this rule. As Khor Kok Peng (*Malaysia's Economy in Decline: What Happened? Why? What to Do?*, 1987) has shown, at least part of the need for increased foreign-exchange earnings can be explained by the rapid expansion of Malaysia's debt, as a result of the development strategy it adopted. However, logging of Malaysian forests is nothing new. Between 1963 and 1985, for example, 2.8 million hectares of tropical forests in the

Sarawak region of Borneo, equivalent to 30% of Sarawak's total forest area, had been logged. And, as if exploitation on this scale were not enough, at the end of 1984, an additional 5.8 million hectares of the total forest area was licensed out for logging.

Malaysia has a majority share in the global trade in tropical logs, amounting to 58% in 1983; of this Sarawak alone accounted for 39% in 1985. Timber is Malaysia's most important foreign exchange earner, and its value to the country's economy — US$1.7 billion in 1986 — is obvious.

Even if the forests were uninhabited, exploitation on such a scale would be questionable at the very least. However, this is simply not the case as Along Saga, a member of the Penan, one of the numerous indigenous tribes, explained: "Before anyone else, and long before the timber company came, we were already on this land. This is the land of our forefathers, and their forefathers before them. But now with just a few years of logging these centuries-old forests are almost finished."

The destruction is not limited simply to cutting down trees. The logging activities have resulted in the disappearance of the forest's plant, food and wildlife resources which were utilised by the Penan. Furthermore, the water systems are clogged with silt, debris and chemicals from the logging activities. Rosylin Nyagong, a 29-year-old mother who is participating in one of the blockades of the loggers' roads into the forest, told Teresa Apin, a researcher based in Penang, what this destruction has meant to the Penan:

"They mowed down our forest and they levelled our hills. The sacred graves of our ancestors were desecrated. Our water and streams are contaminated, our plant life destroyed. And the forest animals are killed or have run away. The forest provides us with wild sago and fruits for food, ten kinds of wood for our blowpipes, and many different types of plants as medicines for headaches, sprains, wounds, and other ailments. We women collect *uwai* (rattan) and *daun* (leaves) to make our shelters and baskets. The forest is our source of survival. Without the forest we'll all be dead and now there's hardly anything left. That's why we'll stay at this blockade till they listen to us. We want them to leave our land."

According to Harrison Ngau, the representative of Friends of the Earth Malaysia in Marudi, the centre of Baram district, years of representation to government officials by the tribespeople achieved little. Ngau says: "These people are very gentle and peaceful by nature. They've resorted to blockades through sheer desperation to defend their rights and property, since official assistance hasn't been forthcoming, despite their crying for help for many years."

In the light of this apparent lack of interest on the part of the authorities, it is no wonder that the tribespeople of Sarawak have taken matters into their own hands. They have blockaded at least 20 logging camps, using logs, wooden structures and their own bodies as barriers. The barricades are guarded day and night by men and women, many of the latter still breastfeeding their children. Their motivation is straightforward; in the words of one man, "We have nothing more to lose." The personal costs of their action have been high. The Penan, for example, are hunter-gatherers but since the blockades began in March 1987, those taking part have had to stop looking for food. This has meant that most of them now eat only one, or at most two, meals daily, and the variety of their food has decreased. Their most common meal now is plain rice and tapioca leaves.

The blockades have already achieved some limited success in securing the tribespeople's demands for a cancellation of timber concessions where operations have not yet started, for fair compensation for those whose land and trees have been damaged by the logging and, most important of all, recognition of traditional land rights. They particularly want the Malaysian government to review the land laws so as to increase the area of protected communal forests and to safeguard their rights to traditional lands and forests from the encroachment of loggers and other outside forces.

For a time during 1987 the blockades successfully paralysed the timber trade in two districts, denying the mostly locally-owned timber companies both access to the logging camps and the logs already cut. This short-term success has thrown the timber trade into turmoil, fearing that it will lose its lucrative foreign markets in the industrialised world. Japan alone takes 61% of exported Malaysian timber.

Nevertheless, the tribespeople face a formidable task if they are to achieve their goals. The April 1987 election in Sarawak revealed the extent to which politicians of both major political parties are involved in the logging operations. It has been these connections, plus the great profitability of logging, which combined to prevent an earlier sympathetic official response to the tribespeople's requests for protection of their land. Nor do they underestimate the problems ahead; but as an elderly Penan woman at one of the blockades told Teresa Apin: "Until we die, we will block this road. I hope you will tell the outside world why."

The increasing effectiveness of the blockade and the publicity which it received have clearly worried the Sarawak state government. During October 1987 the federal government detained without trial 90 individuals from a variety of religious, political, human rights and environmental organisations on the mainland (including CAFOD partners) under the severe Internal Security Act. Taking advantage of this, the Sarawak government moved against the blockade. Harrison Ngau was

Photo: John Payne/ICCE

The continued logging of Sarawak's tropical forests threatens the plant, food and wildlife resources upon which the Penan rely, and pollutes local water supplies.

detained in late October, and by November at least 48 tribal people from the Kenyah, Kayan and Penan groups who had been maintaining the blockades had been arrested and charged with offences which included obstructing the police, wrongful restraint, and, ironically, unlawful occupation of state lands.

Nonetheless, the Malaysian government clearly remained concerned. During a visit to Europe to promote timber exports, which totalled 1.37 million cubic metres to Europe in 1987, the Minister for Primary Industries, Dr Lim Keng Yaik, denied in an interview with the *Financial Times* (19 April 1988) that the logging industry was a threat to the continued existence of his country's tropical rainforests. He strongly defended his government's conservation policies and asserted that Malaysia prided itself on its "sound" forestry policy. The government did not underestimate the problems associated with managing what he described as "one of the most complex, if not the most complex, ecosystems in the world". He expressed the view that the International Tropical Timber Organisation (ITTO) could play a role in this regard by assisting tropical timber producing countries to refine further their rainforest management policies.

This suggestion was received unfavourably at the annual meeting of the ITTO in Rio de Janeiro in June 1988. Representatives of consumer countries argued that the ITTO should not become too involved in projects, some 50 of which were proposed, ranging from forest management research to pilot projects for improving the exchange of market information, since they feared that they would have to bear the cost. This position was supported by some UN bodies, which argued that forest conservation was better handled through the Tropical Forests Action Plan and other already-established agreements. But producer countries and environmental groups strongly opposed this, pointing out that not enough was being done under such plans and that many viewed the Tropical Forests Action Plan as fatally flawed (see p.71, Box 4).

Source: Third World Network Features, Penang, Malaysia.

CHAPTER 3

GREATER WEALTH, GREATER POVERTY: DEVELOPMENT IN PRACTICE

The implementation of development projects and programmes has been a learning process for all concerned. Forty years ago, despite considerable investment in particular areas of third world economies (plantations, mines, and so on) and in the infrastructure (roads, railways, ports etc) required to permit the export of their products to the industrialised world, there was little experience of development. As a result, the early history of development is littered with examples of ill-designed and poorly-implemented projects and programmes. Over time, however, and with increasing experience, these apparently became fewer in number as the checklist of factors to be taken into account in design and implementation grew from the lessons of past mistakes. Here we will attempt to discuss projects and programmes which achieved at least some of their goals. This may well be a limited sample, but the general thrust of our earlier comments has, after all, been to point out the relative failure of the past 40 years of development practice to achieve even the goal of economic growth. Bearing in mind the intimate link between the development process and the environment, it is intended in what follows not only to explore the reasons for this failure, but also to highlight the impact of some projects on the environment.

That there has been such an impact and that in many, if not the majority, of cases it has been negative is undeniable. But this is not to imply that it was the deliberate policy of aid donors to support environmentally damaging projects. On the contrary, the environmental ill effects were due more likely to omission than to commission and, in all probability, they arose from twin causes. Firstly, environmental issues were not in the forefront of donors' minds, if they were present at all. There is little in either modernisation or integration theory which would awaken concern over the environmental impact of projects. Secondly, for a significant part of the period under review, the prevailing attitude of both donors and recipients was that the environment and all that it provided was there to be used. And, it should be noted, for many third world (and other) governments and people that remains the attitude today.

The impact of the development process on the environment is a relatively new concern for those who design projects for many of the larger donors' programmes. Thus, it is only recently that the World Bank formulated a detailed policy on the environmental impact of development and significantly increased the staffing of its

39

A new road cuts through the Amazon forest in San Julian, Bolivia, allowing land to be cleared for the resettlement of highland Indians. The environmental impact of development projects is a relatively new consideration for those who design projects.

Photo: Sean Sprague/Panos Pictures

environmental impact assessment unit (see Appendix 1). Earlier policy, as the Bank implicitly acknowledges, was inadequate. The overwhelming staff bias towards economics graduates meant that concerns which did not appear to be directly related to economic growth tended to be downgraded in importance. The management's determination to right this can be seen in the increased number of environmentalists on the staff (now 65) and the fact that this increase took place during a period of general retrenchment, when over 500 staff, mostly economists, were made redundant. At least part of the Bank's work in the coming years will be associated with correcting the errors of the past — and the relatively late recognition of the failure of earlier policies means that much repair work has to be done.

Nonetheless, a note of caution has to be sounded; as Appendix 1 shows, there is little success to demonstrate at present. The Bank's Environmental Issues Papers were only completed early in 1989, and the other planned work has a far longer timespan. Furthermore, analysis of the first country study to be published — that on Indonesia — shows a marked top-down approach to development, which suggests that there has been little change in the Bank's thinking. Policies, like favoured theories, are also apt to change over time, and so what is needed is continual monitoring of the achievements of these policies in order to assess their validity. This is even more necessary when one considers of the reservations of the Bank's operational staff and their resentment at what they see as a new source of interference in their work.

Similarly, although Britain's Overseas Development Administration (ODA) has for some time had rough guidelines which it applied in the case of environmental issues related to development assistance (see Appendix 2), it has only recently set about formalising these guidelines (the final version was published in March 1989). ODA staff stress that the guideline note was just that — brief guidelines on which responsible staff could draw and expand. Nevertheless, it provides an insight into the environmental concerns which helped determine both project and programme aid choices since 1981. It is important to note that various external constraining factors militated against its full implementation in every case. One of these was financial. The note contains repeated references to "inordinate expense" in the appraisal, monitoring and evaluation phases of projects without properly clarifying what is meant by this. This vagueness leaves open the possibility that cost-conscious staff will prefer to spend a declining ODA budget on projects and programmes rather than on expensive studies.

Similarly, as the then minister himself regularly emphasised, bilateral aid programmes are motivated by a number of factors, of which idealism and ethics are only aspects. Concerns relating to Britain's political or economic advantage are at least as important for the present government in its aid programme as the promotion of the well-being of recipient countries. There need be no conflict where these concerns coincide to the benefit of both parties. One possible outcome is that where British assistance is being considered to a third world country for a project which is favoured by the recipient government and promotes British interests, but which is also damaging to the environment, the project may still be funded.

ODA policy apart, a number of British NGOs have criticised the government's response[8] to the Brundtland report.[9] While recognising this response as a step in the right direction with a number of positive features to its credit, the NGOs express a number of specific reservations, notably regarding the government's failure to examine the sustainability of its economic policies, or to measure their impact on the Third World and improve them where necessary. The government is also criticised for underestimating the effects of adverse international financial conditions and their role in exacerbating environmental degradation throughout the Third World, for failing to promote debt relief for all debtor countries, and for not doing enough to persuade the IMF and the World Bank seriously to consider new policies.

The NGOs have sharp words, too, for what they see as a contradiction between the government's aid and trade policies. It makes no sense, they argue, for the government to say in its Brundtland response that it encourages diversification through its bilateral aid programme, while its other policies — particularly the EC's trade policy — work directly against this, penalising poor countries when they attempt to export basic processed goods (the terms of the Multi-Fibre Arrangement, MFA, relating to textile imports from the Third World and the situations to which they give rise are but one example of this).

Despite their criticisms, the NGOs nevertheless regard the government's response as "a contribution to the public debate on these major issues of our times". And the NGO critique received a positive reaction from the then Minister for Overseas Development, Mr Chris Patten, who recently stated publicly that he was looking forward "to discussing the aid issues raised in their paper with them"[10] — which suggests that at least some government departments are addressing the subject in a serious and constructive manner.

Given the relative "newness" of environmental concern and the resistance to environmental issues still displayed by many third world governments, it must be acknowledged that aid donors are placed in a difficult position. To many of them it must seem that they are in a classic "no-win situation": condemned for interfering in issues internal to the recipient countries if they insist on including environmental issues in aid policy design, and damned for not preventing the foreseeable negative consequences of their programmes and projects if they do not. Thus, even the limited steps taken to date are to be welcomed — and donors should be encouraged to go further and expand their dialogue with recipient governments to convince them of the importance of such considerations.

It seems strange that donors were not alerted to these concerns earlier. For even if one considers environmental questions from a purely economic viewpoint, it is apparent that they ought to play an important, although not necessarily determinant, role in the design of development policy. With the benefit of hindsight, it would seem self-evident that if a development process is to create the conditions necessary for an improved quality of life, it must be sustainable over time. There is little advantage to be had from short-term gains which soon disappear because of soil exhaustion, a depleted resource base or such pollution of the environment that ill-health results. And yet, as the following examples show, these are some of the results of the development policies followed to date. One is forced to ask how this could have ever been regarded seriously as development. We shall return to this question later.

Development in Indonesia

The Indonesian archipelago has a total area of 1,919 square kilometres, possesses more than 10% of the world's tropical forests and is classified by the World Bank (*World Development Report 1988*) as a lower middle-income country. As such, it is considerably better-off than many other third world nations. Its population of over 169 million is culturally diverse. Life expectancy at birth is 56 years. The United Nations Children's Fund (UNICEF) estimates that the annual population growth rate is 2.1% (*The State of the World's Children 1988*, UNICEF).

Java, the most settled island in the archipelago, is home to approximately 65% of the rapidly-growing population. Shortage of land encouraged President Suharto's government to promote the resettlement of Javanese on the other islands — particularly in the territories of Irian Jaya and East Timor, which Indonesia took over in December 1975. The transmigration programme, as the frontier resettlement policy became known, has been funded by the World Bank and other donors from its inception. World Bank support to date totals over US$650 million and a further loan is currently being finalised.

Two underlying reasons explain the government's enthusiasm for the programme. The poverty of many Javanese was seen to be closely connected with their lack of access to land on an overcrowded island. The self-evident solution was to move people from an area of high population density to other parts of the country where the density was significantly lower. Security considerations, however, were equally important, as is suggested by the fact that the military were given the responsibility of overseeing the programme. Underlying the government's security concerns was the controversy surrounding Jakarta's assumption of sovereignty over both East Timor and Irian Jaya. Many of the inhabitants reject Indonesia's claim to these territories and have waged a resistance of varying intensity against what they regard as the Indonesian invasion and annexation. Thus, a significant motivation for the government's promotion of the transmigration programme was the desire to increase the number of loyal Indonesians in that territory.

Not all those resettled were seen as likely peasant farmers. The programme was designed as a mix of commercial exploitation of the forest coupled with smallholding farms; the government considered the area to be uninhabited and it still does not recognise the land rights of local tribespeople.

The environmental impact of the programme has been severe. According to the United Nations Food and Agriculture Organization (FAO) up to 1 million hectares of forest are being destroyed each year through a combination of commercial logging and slash-and-burn agricultural methods. The government points to inappropriate farming methods as the cause. According to President Suharto over 1 million

Indonesian farmers still move from place to place, clearing the rain forest as they go. Such land use patterns have resulted in spectacular ecological disasters. During 1982, a forest fire blazed uncontrolled for nine months, and destroyed 4 million hectares of forest. More recently, the country has experienced a series of floods and landslides, the worst of which occurred during 1987 in West Sumatra and claimed over 100 lives.

Ironically, agricultural modernisation programmes carried out in Java in recent years have done little to eradicate the problems of poorer Indonesians. While these programmes have meant that the country is now self-sufficient in rice, the staple food, the use of high-yielding seed varieties to achieve this has increased the numbers of landless people. Such Green Revolution packages are capital-intensive and beyond the means of poorer farmers (see *Just Food*, CAFOD, 1984). They lose their land either because they sell it for reasons of poverty or because the landowners who had previously rented it to them now see the opportunity of greater profit by farming it themselves. The result, as in other third world countries, has been to speed up the migration of penniless people to the cities. And there they have proved a fertile recruiting ground for the resettlement programme in which they are likely to continue the agricultural practices of which President Suharto was so disapproving.

The real balance of blame for the destruction of the forest is difficult to determine. Although a government ban on the export of unprocessed logs in 1980 forced a number of companies in far-flung provinces to

A surveyor at work on the transmigration project in Kalimantan, Indonesia.

cease operations, the same decision had the opposite effect in Kalimantan, the best source of logs. In this province the ban brought a sharp increase in the number of sawmills and plywood factories as the country sought to compensate for the fall in oil prices by taking advantage of the increased prices of plywood. The result, according to US agronomists, has been an accelerated invasion of the forest. Further difficulties in controlling the amount of commercial logging arise from the fact that many of the logging concessions are allegedly controlled by military holding companies, thereby providing jobs for retired military officers and guaranteeing unofficial sources of finance for the purchase of arms and other military equipment.

In line with its current increased concern for the environmental impact of the projects it funds, the World Bank has acknowledged that mistakes were made in the past. In fact, loans currently being negotiated are to be used for the improvement and rehabilitation of existing sites under the transmigration programme, rather than any expansion. Bank officials point out that the Indonesian government appears to be taking the environmental impact of the programme more seriously now; according to Gloria Davis, head of the Bank's Asia-Pacific Environment Unit, it has targeted 26% of Indonesian forests for conservation, a percentage far higher than in other countries. However, as Ms Davis observes, "the Bank cannot afford to be sanctimonious about it — we, after all, encouraged the government to borrow for the programme".

The Bank is also encouraging Jakarta to improve its procedures for compensating local tribes for their loss of land. As noted before, the government does not recognise the rights of local tribespeople to the land which they occupy, so any compensation is based on tree and crop losses. However, according to aid workers in the areas affected, even this system of compensation is subject to frequent abuse by Indonesian officials — one farmer in Irian Jaya, reported that, when the government decided to take possession of his land to build an airport, he received a string of cowrie shells in compensation. Cowrie shells are traditional currency in the area but have little, if any, exchange value in a modern cash economy.

Concern also exists over the impact of the programme in those areas where ownership is not contested. Land reclamation programmes in swampy areas are causing serious concern for Indonesian and foreign ecologists. They point out that land reclamation frequently results in acid soils, leading to river pollution; this in turn threatens the mangrove swamps downstream of the reclaimed areas and, eventually, the livelihood of local fishermen.

Meanwhile, two further questions must be asked in connection with this programme. Firstly, has it benefited the poorer members of Indonesian society? While it is true that a number of people who would not otherwise have had access to land have received it under the programme, it is not clear that the few who benefited continue to do so. Secondly, and equally important, have the benefits which have accrued to some sections of the population been at the expense of other members of the society?

The short answer is that the transmigration programme and the associated development introduced have had negative effects. The fragile rainforest soil has demonstrated its inability to sustain continued cultivation, thereby denying those who received the land long-term security and an improvement in their quality of life. The popular invasion of the forests encouraged by the programme has resulted in environmental destruction on a massive scale. And, in the short term, the benefits which accrued to one group of Indonesians have been at the expense of others, including indigenous peoples, whom the government also claims are its citizens.

Lastly, one must also ask whether the transmigration project has met even the basic criterion of mainstream development thinking — namely, economic viablity. On this test too, the programme must be said to have failed. The decision to target loans currently under negotiation between the Bank and the Indonesian government towards the regeneration and revitalisation of areas where the programme had already been introduced adds much weight to this point. Nonetheless, the Bank's decision to grasp the nettle and address the inappropriate design of its earlier methodology in this particular project is to be welcomed. Similarly, the government's new-found recognition of the importance of environmental care in its development programme is also to be supported, as the growing Indonesian environmental movement has recognised.

Agricultural development in India

By the beginning of the 1980s, the World Bank's *World Development Report 1981* observed that "agriculture has been given greater emphasis in recent thinking on development". It continued to stress the role of industrialisation as critical to higher productivity and growth but added that, in most countries, the industrialisation process "has been supported by broadly based agricultural progress". The Bank's thinking at this time was summed up as follows:

Agricultural success generates domestic demand for industrial products; supplies cheap food to industrial workers and raw materials for agro-processing; earns foreign exchange to finance imports of capital and intermediate goods for industry; and encourages labour-intensive industries in small towns and villages.

The Indian Punjab was an early testing ground for the validity of such theories. Donors, including the World Bank, USAID, and the ODA, supported agricultural modernisation plans, particularly through the use of Green Revolution technology. This package consists of high responding seed varieties, accompanied by inputs of water (through irrigation), biocides (pesticides, fungicides, and herbicides), and fertilisers, all of which have to be supplied at the optimum moment in order to maximise production. Farmers in the Punjab had begun to become involved in commercial agriculture from the late 1950s, and were thought to be most likely to respond positively to modern agricultural methods because they were more willing to take the financial risks associated with new methods.

As it turned out, the Green Revolution package proved phenomenally successful in the Punjab. Not only did the larger farmers make use of the new seed varieties, but so, too, did smallholders and tenant farmers. Average yields of the crops traditionally grown in the area almost doubled, and farmers soon moved on to producing new crops, including rice and potatoes. The increased farm income led them to invest in the setting up of small industries and service establishments which provided employment for many landless labourers.

The success of the scheme in the Punjab encouraged its extension to other areas of India as well. This required the provision of irrigation facilities through the construction of dams and tube-wells, financed by aid loans. The ample supply of water for those farmers who switched to the new methods led to problems, however. Many of the new wells were sited on land belonging to larger landowners, who claimed that the water made available by the wells belonged to them, and that any other farmers who wished to make use of it had to buy it. A similar situation emerged in respect of the water from the dams which were built.

The construction of dams brought an additional problem because many Indian state governments refused to recognise the land rights of the minority peoples. One of the most renowned is the Narmada Valley Development Scheme, where construction of the first dam in the scheme, Sardar Sarovar in Gujarat state, is expected to be completed in 1995. The dam, 18% financed by the World Bank at a cost of US$300 million (the total cost being US$1,674 million), which represents almost half the foreign-exchange costs of the dam, will displace 70,000 people. In all, the 30 dams envisaged under the scheme will displace around 1.2 million people.

The major stated purpose of the Sardar Sarovar dam is irrigation and the generation of electricity. The project's feasibility study indicated that once the irrigation delivery channels have been completed in 1998, for which the Bank will provide an additional loan of US$150 million (approximately 30% of the required investment), 5 million people in Gujarat will directly benefit. The irrigation of approximately 2 million hectares is expected to increase agricultural production by 40-45%. However, as most of the irrigated land lies in the state's relatively prosperous coastal belt where the majority of the poor are landless labourers (40% of the agricultural workforce), it is difficult to see how they will benefit from the resulting increased production.

In the initial negotiations leading to the agreement to finance the dam's construction, the World Bank failed to ensure that the interests of those displaced were protected. Subsequently, as a result of locally organised pressure, a limited agreement to provide compensation or alternative land was reached. Local representatives say that, on paper, it is one of the most sensitive resettlement agreements ever negotiated. However, they have expressed concern that, while the letter of the agreement may be implemented, its spirit will not. And this fear is supported by the very different interpretation of the Gujarati government's relief and rehabilitation responsibilities revealed in a Supreme Court affidavit filed by the project's Rehabilitation and Land Acquisition Offices.

In spite of the problems associated with the Green Revolution package, it achieved one significant and undeniable success. India, which 30 years ago was believed to be chronically prone to famine, now produces more than enough food for its own needs. This not only allows it to export grain but it has also enabled the government to establish a national reserve for distribution during bad harvest years. One such occurred in 1987, when the country suffered one of the worst droughts in its recent history. Caritas India, CAFOD's partner in the country, made available approximately £6.6 million for drought relief for the people worst affected. Accompanying their request for financial assistance to meet this considerable commitment, Caritas India supplied convincing information on the cause of the drought as being threefold: deforestation; misuse of irrigation water; and over-exploitation of groundwater.

Deforestation. In India the past four decades have seen the disappearance of forests in the now desert-like districts in south-western Rajasthan. The combination of political and economic interests in these areas resulted in such extensive logging that the forests were totally destroyed. This upset the ecological balance. Trees, necessary for water retention and, possibly, for maintaining the local micro-climate, were cut down *en masse*, earning vast profits for the loggers but so upsetting the local environment that it experienced the worst ever famine and drought conditions in its history during 1987.

The Indian government responded by a much publicised re-forestation programme. However, Indian critics of the plan have said that, far from helping the poor, the scheme will only lead to still greater profits for the already rich. Furthermore, they argue that the trees planted under the scheme — eucalyptus, teak and pine — are detrimental to the local environment of the area. Eucalyptus plantations, in particular, use up an excessive amount of groundwater, thereby draining the water table, and their root-spread makes adjacent land unusable for cultivation.

Misuse of irrigation water. In the state of Maharashtra, the vast majority of irrigation water is used by large farms growing sugarcane. This deprives smaller farmers who grow food crops of their fair share of the water available and has resulted in recurring food and drinking water crises in the surrounding villages. The power of the sugar barons is such that for years the Indian government ignored the protests of the poor. More recently, thanks to the support of the Maharashtra Drought Relief and Eradication Committee, the poor farmers have become more vocal in their demands for a fairer distribution of the irrigation water available.

Over-exploitation of groundwater. Tubewells can have serious negative effects as well as providing water for use. Continued draining of water in excess of replenishment makes the water table fall, thereby causing a number of wells to fail. In Maharashtra, between 1960 and 1961, the number of wells increased by 51% while the area irrigated doubled, due mainly to the increased use of mechanised pumps. This constant depletion of available groundwater led to a rise in the number of villages without any source of water from 17,000 in 1980 to 23,000 in 1983. In addition, most of the wells were sunk on privately owned land and more often than not the owners denied others the free use of the water. This situation is common across the whole country; the Indian government itself has become an active participant, sinking tubewells in unlimited numbers in its efforts to meet the needs created by the drought.

One of the most tragic ironies of the situation is the fact that India, although one of the wettest countries in the world, is now also one of the most drought-prone, as well as being subject to flooding as was shown by the floods in the north which killed over 300 people during September 1988. This situation has arisen because of the unbalanced and short-sighted policies followed to date.

Paying the price: Brazil, the debt crisis and emerging ecocide

CAFOD's pamphlet, *Land and Poverty* (1987), described the expanding attack on the Amazon forest within Brazil, Latin America's largest state. As we saw, successive Brazilian governments have encouraged the settlement of the country's Amazon provinces in order to avoid addressing the need for a more just redistribution of the land and to expand foreign-currency earnings through increased exports. The expansion into the Amazon forests has taken place in many areas of economic activity: mining; commercial agriculture and ranching and food production. Peasant farmers too have moved into the region as a direct result of federal government encouragement. Susan George gives examples of such encouragement in her book, *A Fate Worse Than Debt* (1988), in which she quotes government-sponsored advertisements: "We are making the largest agricultural reform in the world" and "Good land, appropriate land...these lands offer excellent possibilities for the expansion of agricultural productivity", which were reportedly brought to an end in 1986.

However, the success achieved by the large landowners, politically organised in the Democratic Rural Union (UDR), in May 1988, when the Brazilian parliament rejected the agrarian reform legislation supported by the Church and the popular movement, suggests that even if the advertisements themselves do not reappear the migration of people will continue unabated. Poor people were not, as we have seen in *Land and Poverty*, the only targets of these advertisements; large individual landowners and corporations were particularly encouraged through tax and other incentives to establish commercial concerns (principally cattle-ranching ventures) so as to increase the country's foreign-exchange earnings.

These ventures, and the foreign-exchange earnings they were expected to generate, were seen by the government to be necessary in the short term so as to maintain the country's creditworthiness until the predicted benefits of the world's largest development scheme, the Grande Carajas Project, became available to solve Brazil's crippling debt. That this view is shared by major international economic agents, is shown not only by the identity of the participants in Grande Carajas, which include the European Community and the World Bank, but also by the agreement of the country's creditors to exempt the scheme from the controls agreed under the various IMF stabilisation programmes and IMF/World Bank-sponsored structural adjustment programmes negotiated with the Brazilian Government.

The estimated total cost of Grande Carajas is US$62 billion. Obviously, no single aid donor or source of investment would be either able or willing to risk this sum of money on a single project. Thus, aid loans on the scale of that of the EC (US$600 million), the World Bank, or the Inter-American Development Bank are a small, though significant, component of the overall cost of the project. Nonetheless, it is a matter of concern that development finance on this scale is used to fund projects which are reliably predicted to have a negative impact on both the environment and the people who inhabit the forest. It is also important to recognise that doubt exists, amongst the funding bodies themselves, about the timescale of any financial benefits arising from the project.

Susan George's work illustrates these points well. She points to the Polonoreste Project, located in the western Amazon states of Acre and Rondonia and funded by the World Bank. At present this project has resulted in the deforestation of an area the size of Great Britain. Deforestation on this scale is not confined to this one project, however. The combination of commercial agriculture and the infrastructural development necessary for the level of mineral exploitation required by Grande Carajas has destroyed the Amazon forest in these areas too.

This is by no means the most serious immediate impact. José Lutzenberger, one of Brazil's foremost agronomists and environmentalists, in his testimony before the US Congress in September 1984, lamented the impact of such development on Brazil's Amerindians and on society at large:

Burning forests in Rondonia, Brazil. In ten years most of the state's forest has been cleared by settlers and ranchers.

Photo: Marcos Santilli/Panos Pictures

Their knowledge of the ecology of the forest, their skills in knowing how to use it are lost even before we can register them. The loss of these cultures is just as irreversible as the loss of a species. A species is the result of millions of years of irreversible organic evolution. An indigenous culture is the result of thousands of years of living in harmony with the ecosystem.

For Brazil's Amerindians the threat of cultural, if not physical, extinction is immediate. For Brazilian and world society as a whole, the effect is incalculable. It is unquestionable that we shall have lost something whose potential value we are unaware of at present. Two World Bank staff members have noted that the predicted loss of between 15% and 20% of the world's plant and animal species by the year 2000 could well have very serious side-effects on all our lives, as they have "tremendous future potential as renewable sources of energy, industrial products, medications, genetic inputs to agriculture, and applied agricultural research".

At the beginning of 1988, José Lutzenberger explained the extent of environmental destruction in Brazil alone:

Ten years ago, the state of Rondonia, which is about the size of the United Kingdom, was virgin tropical rainforest with some 10% of the

51

area made up of natural savannahs and swamps. It is likely that it will be totally devastated by about 1990. Most of the cleared forest has already been abandoned. On the poor forest soils, settlers and ranchers can only survive by cutting down more forest every year. Some of the large plantations of perennial crops such as rubber, cocoa and coffee were a total loss. Hordes of settlers are now resettling in the neighbouring state, Acre. The same destructive process has started there, and will probably not be stopped. Satellite pictures show that in the Amazon region as a whole about 100,000 square kilometres of forest are now destroyed annually.

Such unquantified potential costs are not the only questionable elements of Brazilian development programmes supported by foreign donors. An important part of Grande Carajas is the Tucurui Dam, designed to provide the power for all aspects of the scheme. However, as the World Bank has noted: "When forests...are cleared, reservoirs often become much shallower due to sediment. As a result less electricity can be generated (because less water can flow through the turbines)."

Deforestation destroys the stability of the soil, permitting its erosion and loss into rivers, harbours and canals. The resulting sediment in dams can reduce their useful lifespan by as much as two-thirds, throwing into question the economic costing of whole projects and hence the extent of any projected benefit even in traditional analytical terms.

Growing international concern at the extent of destruction of the Amazon forest prompted the Brazilian government to announce both

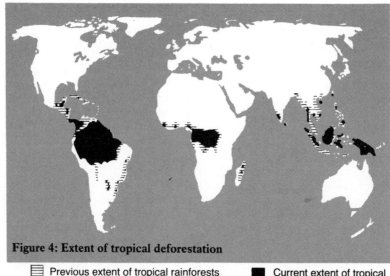

Figure 4: Extent of tropical deforestation

▤ Previous extent of tropical rainforests   ■ Current extent of tropical rainforests

Source: *World Resources 1988-89*, World Resources Institute/ International Institute for Environment and Development/ UNEP (Basic Books, 1988)

an end to its sponsorship of the colonisation programme and the introduction of conservation measures in September 1988. This announcement was quickly rendered meaningless, however, as budgetary cuts forced by the need to service the debt led to the closure of the ministry responsible for the care of the area.

However, the decision to end the colonisation programme was deeply resented by some sections of Brazilian society, which accused environmentalists such as José Lutzenberger and Francisco "Chico" Mendes, leader of the National Rubbertappers Association, founder of the Union of Forest Peoples and a founder member of the Brazilian Workers Party, of encouraging external interference in Brazilian affairs because of their international campaigns to publicise the forest's destruction. This resentment ran so deep that Mendes was murdered in December 1988. UDR supporters have been accused of instigating his murder because they wanted the government to reverse its decision to end support for the colonisation of the Amazon. This would have the effect of reducing popular pressure for agrarian reform and allow large landowners to continue to receive government subsidies for cattle ranching and similar projects in the Amazon region, despite the doubts surrounding their sustainability both in economic as well as environmental terms.

Notes

8. *Brundtland in the Balance: A Critique of the UK Government's Response to the World Commission on Environment and Development*, World Development Movement, (London, February 1989).

9. *Our Common Future. A Perspective by the United Kingdom on the Report of the World Commission on Environment and Development*, Department of the Environment on behalf of the UK Government (London, July 1988).

10. "Common Future — Common Challenge: British Aid Policy and the Environment", address to Cambridge series on the Environment and Development, February 1989.

CHAPTER 4

ENVIRONMENTAL CRITIQUES OF THE DEVELOPMENT MODEL

An Overview

Some of the most trenchant criticisms of conventional development practice advanced by the environmental movement have stressed the shortcomings of the exclusive focus on economic growth which is the cornerstone of accepted development thinking. Michael Redclift and Jonathan Porritt (*Why Bankrupt the Earth? An Exploration into International Economics and the Environment*, 1986) provide what is possibly the clearest exposition to date of current thinking on the environment and development originating in the environmental movement in the industrialised world. They observe:

> *Many claims have been made in the name of "development": the eradication of poverty, the meeting of basic needs, the narrowing of the gap between North and South. Little has been achieved, even when measured by conventional economic indicators such as economic growth and income per person. Moreover, the contemporary model of development has progressively eroded the global environment and mortgaged the future of many less developed countries.*

This may well overstate the case. As noted in the Chapter 1, there have been improvements in the situation of many of the Third World's people — increased life expectancy, improved access to health care and education and, not least, recognition by aid donors of the importance of care for the environment. These are not small achievements. And to them should be added the emergence of former aid recipients, principally South Korea and Singapore, as major economic agents and the significant achievement of India which, in the space of 20 years, has changed from a country in which famine was believed to be endemic to one self-sufficient in food production. On the negative side of the coin, sub-Saharan Africa appears caught in a time-loop, with production levels declining in per capita terms, and even in absolute terms in some countries. Overall, however, the past 40 years have witnessed some limited improvement in the quality of life enjoyed by most people.

Nonetheless, such hard-won improvements are under threat as third world governments seek to service their debts by increasing their exports and reducing their spending. Redclift and Porritt argue forcefully that it is the model itself which has led to the present crisis in development and that "no lasting solutions will be found until a very different set of economic priorities is introduced". Their critique was seminal. It represented a major attempt to integrate the main themes of the environmental movement's criticisms into an analysis of the global economy. It remains in the forefront of the critique advanced by the environmental movement today, representing the most succinct exposition of the links between development and the environment by such campaigning groups in Britain and, possibly, the industrialised

Spraying insecticides on mango trees, India. Environmentalists have criticised the widespread use of biocides and fertilizers in agriculture, which often increase crop yields at the expense of polluting water supplies and increasing health risks.

Photo: Ron Gilling/Panos Pictures

world generally. In the light of this, it is clearly important to consider their arguments in some detail and to discuss the most important questions arising at greater length.

Four areas of criticism
Redclift and Porritt point to four main factors — the role of trade relations, the role of aid, the debt crisis, and the impact of transnational corporations — arguing that each has militated against the possibility of true development in third world countries.

1. *The trading relationship.* Trade theory, such as that developed by David Ricardo, contends that, under a regime of fairly free international trade, the gains which accrue to all parties will outweigh any losses. Consequently the development model has stressed the importance of trade between countries and has promoted the production of exports for sale in the international market. But the export possibilities of many third world countries are limited to unprocessed or semi-processed mineral or agricultural commodities. It is only in a relatively few cases, for example the East Asian newly industrialising countries (NICs) of South Korea, Taiwan, Hong Kong and Singapore, that third world countries have developed an industrial base which has enabled them to compete on equal terms with producers of similar products in the industrialised countries. The experience of most third world countries has been concisely summed up by former Tanzanian president, Julius Nyerere: "The primary producing countries are price takers, not price makers. We sell cheap and we buy dear whether we like it or not."

Redclift and Porritt question the emphasis placed by the international financial institutions and official donors on export-led growth. They assert that the experience of Latin American countries in this regard has been universally negative, resulting in dramatically increased levels of sovereign debt and impossible levels of debt service. Africa was also recommended by the World Bank's Berg Report (1981) to follow the path of export-led growth, and although later World Bank reports have placed greater emphasis on developing food security on the continent, they too have repeatedly stressed the need to increase exports of agricultural products in order to increase foreign-exchange earnings. Redclift and Porritt note that many African governments have commented on the apparent contradiction between such recommendations from the World Bank and the IMF and the practice of industrialised countries in trying to limit their imports.
According to Redclift and Porritt, the emphasis on economic growth has had extremely serious environmental consequences. For example, the effort to increase agricultural production has led to topsoil losses through over-cropping, scarcity of fresh water through the depletion of groundwater, the deterioration of grasslands through overgrazing, and deforestation. The examples of development projects cited earlier

Box 1: Different arguments

Redclift and Porritt present two contrasting arguments. On the one hand, they express serious reservations about the possibility of export-led growth resulting in sustainable development for all peoples, and in particular for those in third world countries. However, this misses the point. They have failed to identify the importance of internal power relationships, which do much to explain why the growth of Latin American gross domestic product has not benefited all Latin Americans. Trickle-down may not work in practice but the reasons for its failure are far more complex than the simple North/South divide which the authors appear to accept as the cause.

On the other hand, having questioned the benefits of trade as the vehicle for development, they then appear to accept the arguments of free-traders, who contend that it is the protectionist barriers erected by governments which distort the operations of the market, thereby depriving some producers of the benefits of trade. It should be pointed out that this argument is in total contradiction to the first — that export-led growth strategies advocated by the World Bank and others have resulted in the underdevelopment of third world countries and the progressive impoverishment of their peoples.

The difficulty is common to many liberal critics of conventional development theory and practice. They appear to argue in favour of self-sufficient development, viewing the economy of a country in isolation from the global economy and yet they also emphasise the unfairness of the international trade regime, pointing in particular to barriers to trade in third world products, particularly where these are processed. This emphasis implicitly accepts the integration of national economies into the international economy.

Clearly, the facts of the case makes the first argument a non-starter. Countries exist within a global economy and to view them in isolation from it is to ignore the facts. And, equally importantly, this argument misses the point. Trade is not anti-developmental; on the contrary, it provides by far the largest part of a country's foreign-exchange earnings. The question which should be addressed is not whether there should be trade but who should determine the terms of trade and the products to be traded. If a country's production is determined by outside forces, rather than by its domestic needs, then any benefits resulting from that production and the subsequent trade in it will be is subject to the vagaries of the purchasers. In other words, the choice of products traded should be decided by domestic needs and what it is possible to produce.

support at least some of these points.

However, it should be pointed out that many of the examples cited, as well as those which underpin the analysis by Redclift and Porritt, are inevitably drawn from a period prior to the new emphasis placed by the World Bank and other donors on environmental issues in development project design. The true test of Redclift and Porritt's contention is whether policies designed to encourage economic growth necessarily result in environmental degradation and, if they do, how much degradation can be tolerated without unacceptable costs to the environment as a whole.

Redclift and Porritt are conscientious in taking up the question of people's impact on the environment. As we have seen, in many instances poor people have been an immediate cause of environmental destruction. Nevertheless, as they note, increased population pressure alone cannot adequately explain why people who have long-standing traditions of care for their environment suddenly engage in practices which result in its destruction. Redclift and Porritt are punctilious in their efforts to outline the causes of overgrazing, for example. They point to the efforts of aid donors to monetise local economies. In the case of pastoralists, they point out that both official aid donors and governments have encouraged pastoralists to settle permanently. However desirable and commendable such efforts are, the net effect is to limit the area available for stock to graze. And this has resulted in reductions in both grazing and stock quality and, in the longer term, degradation of the grazing area itself. In its turn, this has effectively destroyed the long-term future of the activity as a source of income for both the pastoralists and the country as a whole.

2. *Aid policy.* Redclift and Porritt argue that aid, and especially bilateral aid, is not provided principally for the alleviation of poverty. On the contrary, they contend that its purpose is largely twofold: to gain political advantage in the global power struggle and to guarantee financial rewards by tying the provision of aid to the purchase of goods supplied by the donor. Aid, they argue, does not go "to those who need it most: but to those whom we (the donors) *choose*, usually *when they need it least*, after the damage has been done" (their emphasis).

Non-emergency food aid, in particular, is severely criticised for the deleterious effect it has on people and their environment. Citing an Oxfam publication (Tony Jackson with Deborah Eade: *Against the Grain: The Dilemma of Food Aid*, 1982) — which concludes that such food aid is "a particularly cumbersome and inappropriate means of providing assistance" and that its "inherent weaknesses have been largely overlooked" — they argue that it has "little to do with development, and even less to do with *sustainable* development". Leaving aside for the moment the accuracy of this argument, it is worth observing that the experience of many developing countries which have followed export-led growth strategies has been that, while exports have

Box 2: Possible uses for non-emergency food aid

The suggestion that a country should emphasise the production of certain products and use the proceeds from their sale to purchase food is not inherently inappropriate. It does assume, however, that the country will be able to earn enough to pay both for the resulting imports and for the goods it needs to promote its development — a condition which, as Redclift and Porrit correctly point out, is seldom met. But just because serious criticisms can be levelled against the provision of non-emergency food aid — as they have been by a number of NGOs, including CAFOD and Christian Aid — there is no reason why the practice should be abandoned altogether. Considerable improvements have been made recently — particularly noteworthy is Ghana's internationally-supported Programme of Action to Mitigate the Social Costs of Adjustment (PAMSCAD) — in the light of which the whole matter deserves to be reconsidered.

Hans Singer and Simon Maxwell, of the University of Sussex's Institute of Development Studies, are of the opinion that it can play a positive role, especially during periods of economic adjustment. If it is well targeted, they point out, it can be used to protect vulnerable groups — the unemployed, women and children — from the worst effects of such necessary adjustment. There are clearly difficulties associated with this, notably in ensuring that it really is the vulnerable who benefit and that the food made available does not lead to greater dependency. But these are matters which relate to the question of what is appropriate under particular circumstances, or to technical questions of distribution, rather than to general positions for or against this type of aid.

increased, so have imports, particularly food imports.

But this has at least as much to do with the type of products produced for export and the factors which have led to this choice. Susan George, for example, argues that such decisions are based on the interests of elites in both industrialised and third world countries so as to maintain economic relationships which work to their mutual advantage. It is equally possible that when faced with the need to increase foreign-exchange earnings, development planners and third world governments take the easiest option — to increase production of a commodity of which there is experience in the country and for which there is an established market. This latter argument does not disprove George's analysis. On the contrary, it may be easier to take this choice because of elite interests in third world and industrialised countries.

The specifically environmental impact of aid projects relates directly to the recommended export-led growth strategy. Redclift and Porritt note that US environmentalist, Bruce Rich, has pointed out that the vast majority of export-oriented agricultural projects which are financed by the multilateral development banks (the World Bank and the regional development banks) involve "the spraying of vast areas with massive amounts of hard pesticides that are often banned in Western countries". Other types of projects funded involve "the construction of big hydro-power and perennial irrigation schemes which require the removal of large populations on to infertile land, with no proper compensation, and which must inevitably lead to widespread waterlogging and soil salinisation as well as the spread of water-borne diseases".

According to a number of writers on environment and development including the director of the British-based Panos Institute, Jon Tinker, and academic authors writing for journals such as the *Canadian Journal of Zoology*, projects to halt the advance of environmental degradation in Africa barely receive consideration. The lack of attention formerly paid to environmental issues in Burkina Faso had resulted in such despair amongst aid agency personnel, according to a *New York Times* report of 29 November 1984, that the World Bank privately circulated suggestions that the time had come to stop investing in the parched north of that country and, instead, to encourage people to migrate south to lands newly-cleansed of diseases such as river blindness.

Redclift and Porritt suggest that much of the environmental degradation which has occurred in the Sahel is now irreversible. They point out that land under vegetation absorbs more heat than bare, sandy soil. This causes more vigorous thermal undercurrents which take up the moisture provided by the plants to higher altitudes where it condenses and falls as rain. Remove the plant cover and the environment stabilises into a state of cooler, bare soil, lower rainfall, and sparser vegetation. The same thought was expressed, if somewhat more cautiously, in *The Times* 18 October 1985: "Although the verdict is not wholly certain it is possible that parts of the western Sahel have already switched to a new lower rainfall regime". As we shall see in Chapter 5, Africa's governments and people refuse to subscribe to this bleak view.

3. *The debt crisis.* The origins and human costs of the debt crisis and the measures suggested to enable countries to service their debts have been discussed fully in *Debt and Poverty* (CAFOD, 1987) and in a number of CAFOD publications, as well as those of other organisations. As we have already observed, the conventional development model was associated with the increasing indebtedness of third world countries. More immediately, the dramatic rise in the oil price caused the massive increase in borrowing by third world countries during the 1970s, and the advent of high real interest rates brought about by the industrialised countries, led by the United States, was the primary cause of the

reduction of global economic growth. This reduced third world foreign-exchange earnings and dramatically increased their countries' debt-service burden, thus precipitating the crisis. While global economic growth has recovered somewhat since 1983/84, the debts of third world countries continue to spiral out of control as their inability to service them results in capitalisation of interest in the numerous debt reschedulings and still further borrowing.

As Redclift and Porritt point out, the strategies devised to manage the debt crisis are, to put it simply, "more of the same". Except in the case of those sub-Saharan African countries which qualify for the assistance agreed at the 1988 Berlin meetings of the IMF and World Bank, such strategies take it for granted that the debt should be serviced, and suggest an increase in exports as the means by which this might be achieved. Thus, agriculture becomes more export-oriented and capital-intensive, which requires greater amounts of foreign exchange. Redclift and Porritt illustrate their argument by referring to the debt crisis facing US farmers: having been encouraged by the banks to borrow to buy more land, machinery and so on, US family farmers, unable to service their loans, are now being driven to produce more and more in order to remain solvent (which has profound environmental consequences), or else they are going bankrupt, only to find themselves forced off the land.

Such an approach to agriculture, Redclift and Porritt suggest, runs counter to common sense. At its root, they claim, lies the unreasonable belief that the fertility of the soil is sustainable in the face of constant over-exploitation; that, in the face of all the evidence, pesticides have at worst a relatively neutral effect; and that continually maximising production will not negatively affect production rates in the future. Farmers themselves, naturally, do not believe this but their financial backers would appear to do so. At least, either they believe it or they are so concerned with short-term profit that they do not consider the long-term results of their demands for repayment.

Redclift and Porritt's concerns also appear applicable at an international level. Continual demands to service their debts in full at all costs ensure that third world governments over-exploit their countries' natural resources in an attempt to maintain their international creditworthiness. Alongside the continuing emphasis on export-oriented agriculture, this strategy demands the maximum exploitation of all saleable resources. Forests are logged with little thought for the future. Mineral extraction is maximised, as is industrial production, with minimal environmental safeguards. The sole concern would appear to be the need to accumulate sufficient foreign exchange to service the debt — and even this is often to no avail.

4. *The impact of transnational corporations.* Redclift and Porritt note that transnational corporations (TNCs) have been severely criticised in recent years for taking a short-term view which puts profit ahead of

nature conservation and human livelihoods, but they take the view that such criticism misses the target, since this is essentially a systematic and rational way for TNCs to operate. Failure to recognise this, they argue, results in misconceived criticism of the ethics of less developed countries (LDCs) governments in making profits out of their hardwood exports without referring to the narrow range of choices available to LDC governments given their international bankruptcy and the external control of *their* food systems by TNCs (emphasis in the original).

Further developing this theme, they point out that in almost all instances TNC agribusiness operations rely on laboratory-bred crops which require large inputs of fertilisers and biocides in order to maximise production. Arguing that this is necessary for agribusiness if it is to be competitive in the international market, they point to the result being a reduction in the flexibility and risk avoidance essential to successful peasant agriculture. Examples of such a reduction in choices available to peasant farmers include single cropping, reduced fallow periods and increased migration to less fertile soils.

Possibly the clearest example of agribusiness penetration of third world agriculture and its environmental impact has been the invasion and destruction of tropical forests. The past 25 years have seen over a quarter of Central America's tropical rainforests destroyed and the land put under grass for beef ranching. Nearly all the beef produced has gone to supply US hamburger chains; by 1981 the US was importing 800,000 tonnes of beef annually at a price less than half that obtained by US beef producers, whereas in 1960 it hardly imported any beef at all. The scale of such exports from Central American countries has meant that, according to an article in *Environment*, "the average domestic cat in the United States now consumes more beef than the average Central American". The emphasis on beef production as a source of foreign exchange for Latin American countries can be seen in the quantity of development aid delivered for this purpose. In the 1970s alone, the World Bank and the regional Inter-American Development Bank made available over US$10 billion for the development of cattle ranching.

The picture is similar in other continents, although in both Africa and Asia the emphasis has been on timber production rather than ranching. Redclift and Porritt acknowledge that the primary reason for the destruction of tropical forests is economic. According to the Brundtland Commission, eight third world countries earn between them US$100 million a year from timber exports. Earning foreign exchange is not only the purpose of third world governments' policies, it is inherent in the development model advocated by official aid donors. The debt crisis has added to the pressures facing third world countries, as creditor institutions have underlined the need to maximise foreign-exchange earnings. Under such conditions, therefore, third world governments are unlikely to be able effectively to implement

Mechanised pineapple-harvesting on a TNC plantation in the Philippines. Many third world governments tolerate the environmental effects of TNC operations because of the foreign-exchange earnings they produce.

Photo: Ron Gilling/Panos Pictures

policies which have other considerations to the fore.[11]

Ironically, the need for foreign exchange is compounded by the need for more food. Thus, for financially bankrupt governments the sparsely-populated wilderness areas, whose conservation is now an important concern for the World Bank (see Appendix 1), represent wasted and unproductive land. Barber Conable has commented on the difficulties now often experienced by Bank officials in their efforts to encourage third world governments to pay greater attention to the environmental impact of development projects. This is particularly the case with those governments which prefer not to take up the challenge of land redistribution within their countries. Frontier colonisation then becomes a national goal, the importance of which transcends almost all other concerns.

Redclift and Porritt argue that earlier critiques from the environmental movement, which focused on the "careless" use of technology as the cause of the resulting environmental degradation, fail to understand the essential, if short-sighted, rationale of those implementing such schemes. They point out that schemes such as those implemented in Brazil or Mexico produce a few crops destined for distant markets, transplant peasants from other parts of the country (often as casual labour), use technology developed in temperate climatic zones and "concentrate decision-making at the centre while passing on the risks to the colonisers". Such risks may well include pollution:

An agricultural project may require extensive irrigation and the control of pests by chemical pesticides...The irrigation scheme is likely to bring with it an incidence of water-borne parasites and pesticides [and] may make insect disease vectors resistant to insecticides. The net result could well be a worsening of the quality of life rather than an improvement. The underlying rationality of such schemes rests in the short-term maximisation of profit, in part, at least, arising from the transference of the risks associated with the schemes to those who are implementing them — the permanent and seasonal labourers.

Nor are these the only pollution risks attached to such schemes. Evidence of leaching of nitrates from fertilisers into the water system is fairly widespread in both third world and industrialised countries. The resultant rapid increase in aquatic plant growth has seen the deoxygenation of rivers and their inability to support life, such as has occurred in East Anglia and elsewhere. Furthermore, pesticides, fungicides and herbicides have also been found in rivers, many of which are a source of food for fish and of water for local communities. The health risks to people drinking water polluted in this way are obvious. But there are clear nutritional effects, as communities which depend on fish as their main source of protein now face reduced catches and therefore increases in the price of fish. Those fish which are caught contain, in some cases at least, significant levels of poisons or poisonous heavy metals such as mercury, in their systems.[12]

Although representative in many ways of the analytical position of the mainstream environmental movement in Western industrialised countries, Redclift and Porritt do not take their analysis far enough. We have already indicated two such shortcomings. One is their failure to investigate adequately the power relationships which exist within third world countries (although it must be acknowledged that they address this question with respect to land distribution issues) and the coincidence of interest between the elite in these countries and the elite in the industrialised countries. Further enquiry here would do much to make good shortcomings in their analysis of the impact of economic growth. Secondly, their understanding of the role which trade could play appears flawed (see Box 1).

Growth, no-growth and appropriate growth
Redclift and Porritt's concept of what constitutes a "good" society also has to be questioned. As they appear to conceive of this, current levels of economic development have either achieved all that should be achieved or have possibly gone too far, at least in certain sectors. Thus, they would seem to be arguing either for a standstill or for a reduction in economic growth.[13] As we have seen, they recognise that substantial numbers of people are currently excluded from the benefits of the wealth already produced. Hence, they argue for a redistribution of existing global resources so as to ensure a decent quality of life for all. A specific example of this is their repeated, and soundly based,

condemnation of the failure of third world governments to address rapidly and constructively the need for land redistribution and provide the necessary support to the beneficiaries. In economic terms, such a programme would amount to an effective redistribution of the capital base of many third world economies.

At an international level, various schemes for such capital redistribution could be devised. One of the means which suggests itself is an international agreement on a commodity pricing policy reflecting the real value of third world products. Inevitably, this would result in increased real prices for third world commodities. Taken to its logical conclusion, any such redistribution would most likely result in a reduction of the quality of life of the majority of residents of industrialised countries, as a result of substantially increased costs of raw materials, food and so on.

This is not to question the fundamental justice of increased prices for the products of many third world countries or the injustice of the means used to keep prices low in many instances. As we have noted earlier, prices of third world goods are determined not by their producers but by the rich and powerful. Prices paid to producers are kept low in a number of ways but amongst the most common are abysmally low wages and woefully inadequate pollution controls, which result in the contamination of water systems and, often, of the land itself by poisonous wastes. It seems elementary justice that those who, impose such costs, however indirectly, should bear the expense associated with the establishment of a more just system.

Equally, one could re-examine the components of "growth". As it is currently measured, a country's gross domestic product (GDP, the total wealth produced) includes a number of items — garbage collection, hospital services, the police and army, for example — which, were the need for them reduced, would leave us all better off. Take hospital services, for example. A healthier population would obviously be better off but would also require fewer such services. Conversely, current measurement of GDP undervalues or ignores a number of positive features. Included in these are things such as domestic work and child care, production not measured in monetary value, or the welfare arising from a peacefully-functioning community due to the unpaid efforts of members of that community. It may be desirable, therefore, that GDP should be calculated by adding together all such positive aspects and viewing the negative features, including environmental degradation, as a charge to be subtracted from the total.

But one is forced to ask who in third world countries would benefit from such price increases or new definitions of growth and GDP, and who would bear the brunt of them in the industrialised world, should either ever be politically feasible. If Susan George's analysis is accurate, comprehensive agrarian reform in third world countries would not necessarily result in the fundamental structural changes which Redclift and Porritt argue are necessary for a more just international economic order. Indeed, the pattern of wealth distribution in many industrial countries is grossly unequal, although the provision of social security benefits has ensured that the poverty which exists is more relative than absolute.

What must be questioned, therefore, is Redclift and Porritt's world-view. Their analysis of the global economy and their resulting desired end-state appear to be essentially static. They appear to believe that if only the existing resources were distributed in a just manner, there would be no need for further economic growth in the world economy. And they also appear to believe that economic growth is fundamentally undesirable because it necessarily results in environmental degradation which cannot be tolerated.

Because such a world-view is shared by many environmentalists, it is important that its theoretical implications should be explored in some depth. In particular two points should be considered. First, whether the present level of wealth in the world is adequate to guarantee an acceptable quality of life for all in the foreseeable future and, equally importantly, whether economic growth *per se* results in intolerable environmental destruction.

i. *Wealth and population growth*. As the environmentalists themselves acknowledge, the existing population growth rate (which, ironically, is largely the result of development successes to date, as it demonstrates a significant rise in life expectancy) places pressure on the environment in which people live. Redistribution of the world's resources in favour

Box 3: Current and projected global population size and growth rates

Region	Population in billions			% Annual Growth Rate		
	1985	2000	2025	1950-1985	1985-2000	2000-2025
World	4.8	6.1	8.2	1.9	1.6	1.2
Africa	0.56	0.87	1.62	2.6	3.1	2.5
Latin America	0.41	0.55	0.78	2.6	2.0	1.4
Asia	2.82	3.55	4.54	2.1	1.6	1.0
North America	0.26	0.30	0.35	1.3	0.8	0.6
Europe	0.49	0.51	0.52	0.7	0.3	0.1
USSR	0.28	0.31	0.37	1.3	0.8	0.6
Oceania	0.02	0.03	0.04	1.9	1.4	0.9

Source: *World Population Prospects: Estimates and Projections as Assessed in 1984*, Department of International Economic and Social Affairs, UN (New York, 1986).

of the majority of the world's population would, arguably, reduce this pressure for a time. However, it is questionable whether such a timespan would be long enough to allow for the necessary change in popular attitudes which would result in significantly lower rates of population increase. Both the overall youth of the world's population and the time lag required between improvements in life security and a reduction in average family size mitigate against this.

Experience has shown that the factors most likely to produce a decline in the rate of population growth are improved financial security and an increase in the level of women's educational attainment. The latter is probably crucial. Not only has it been shown to increase the earning potential of the individual but it also has the inevitable effect of raising the age when women become mothers and, therefore, reducing their period of active fertility. It has also been found to encourage birth spacing, as mothers understand better the nutritional advantages of having fewer children. Nevertheless even with such improvements in financial security and female educational levels, the overall youth of the world's population means that population will continue to expand for the foreseeable future.

Against this background it is therefore questionable whether redistribution alone can guarantee a decent quality of life for all at present and, more importantly, in the future. Some level of economic growth appears necessary, even if only to maintain post-redistribution standards of living. However, this raises questions of equity and political sustainability. Is it equitable to insist on the maintenance of even post-redistribution standards of living and how is this to be done? People would justifiably expect further improvements in their quality of life in order to ensure their continuing individual development. To help this process, some level of economic growth greater than that required for a simple maintenance of any post-redistribution *status quo* would also appear to be necessary.

However, while current rates of population growth are a legitimate area of concern, it is inappropriate to lay too much stress on this as a cause of environmental degradation. As Ed Dommen, of UNCTAD's Inter-Sectoral Issues Unit, points out:

It seems that it is not so much the peasant women who are responsible for the disappearance of the forests around their villages, but the urban population on whose behalf the countryside is scoured.

Hence, the most immediate threat to the environment is posed by the consumer society. And this is particularly true with regard to the use (or misuse) of resources in the industrialised world. According to Dommen: "It is said that the average [North] American baby will consume [during his or her life] as much as an entire Indian village." Consumption on this scale is not only grossly inequitable it is quite simply unsustainable, and to overemphasise the environmental threat posed by population growth in the Third World is to risk distracting attention from the urgent need to address consumption patterns in the industrialised world.

ii. *Necessary environmental degradation?* Furthermore, the question of whether economic growth necessarily results in environmental degradation must be addressed. That it will have an effect on the environment is not in dispute but it is more open to doubt whether this effect is always negative and permanent, and, even when it is both, whether this could not be tolerated over time. As we will see in Case Study 3 at the end of this chapter, economic growth is one of the objectives of the CAFOD-supported Mogoraib-Forto integrated development project, and of the Cape Verde reforestation programme funded by the European Development Fund and the UN Environment Programme. These projects will undoubtedly affects environment in those areas where they are implemented. However, one has to question whether these effects will be negative since the projects' success is founded upon environmental conservation and regeneration. Clearly, there appear to be instances where economic growth can be achieved in a sustainable manner, and there are several other examples given in this book which suggest that these are not unique cases.

But what of the cases where the impact on the environment is negative? Redclift and Porritt would presumably reject these out of hand as unacceptable. But to rule out a project *a priori* for environmental reasons alone is surely as shortsighted as to appraise it in exclusively economic terms. Would it not be better to assess the environmental effects of each individual project in terms of the human — and even environmental — cost of its *not* going ahead? This would give the appraisal of projects a much wider base than has been used to date. One of the reasons why the current drive for growth so often proves unsustainable and fails to achieve even its most limited objectives is that development planners fail to consider a project in all its aspects — anthropological, cultural, economic, environmental, political and social.

Third world critiques

Such views reverberate through the many critiques of development policies advanced by third world environmentalists and development practitioners. This thinking is perhaps most advanced in Asia. In India, for example, both the Chipko (tree-hugging) movement and the more recently formed and academic-based Lokayan, which describes itself as an anti-development thinktank, are severely critical of the development programmes which the country has experienced. The development process in India, they argue, has resulted in man-made floods, drought and desertification. The entire process, in the form of mining, of modern irrigation which depends on dams and tubewells, of forests that are cut down, and of agriculture dependent on chemical fertilisers and pesticides, is causing the damage.

According to Rajni Kothari, a leading figure in Lokayan, the only way to put a stop to this process is "to put a ceiling limit on development", at least development as it is understood in terms of conventional wisdom. Such development, according to another Lokayan member, Professor Dhirubhai Seth, is a "permanent promise which cannot be realised, an illusion in which everyone participates". Critics such as these reject the notions of both "Third World" and "South" because, in their view, these imply that the countries thus grouped together "must catch up with the First and Second worlds (the West and the Communist bloc)", also collectively known as the North. What is needed, according to Seth, is a "fourth type of society that must arise from the untouchables of development".

For these groups development as it is currently implemented, rather than lifting India into the ranks of the affluent, is seen as the latest and most ruthless form of colonial exploitation. The new colonialists are the country's expanding middle class, both rural and urban, who profit from industry and advanced agriculture without paying the costs. As Kothari puts it: "Their allies in this are politicians and officials, including the corrupt local police who are sent out to confront the ecology demonstrators. The whole process is kept in motion by the developed world through aid, investment and trade." Susan George argues in a similar vein. She believes that ordinary people in both North and South should join forces in order to ensure that they, rather than the already rich and powerful, benefit from development.

But criticism such as this is not directed only against official aid donors. Some non-governmental organisations (NGOs) which have been drawn into service by government agencies as a more efficient "delivery service for [this] development" are also targets for criticism. Gustavo Esteva, a Mexican economist, believes that, while "many NGOs had collected the best rhetoric of the fifties and sixties — the clamour for popular participation, decentralisation and local control and the new concept of eco-development", the reality was more of the same. The rhetoric was "a new wrapping that gives the old myth a more poisonous effect". He therefore believes that the world recession was, perversely, something to be welcomed in that it provided the opportunity for "us to protect ourselves and deconstruct the whole development delusion". What is needed, according to Chilean economist, Manfred Maxneef, are the conditions which will permit "a society which can reproduce itself without destroying itself". Third world countries have to work towards achieving "a coherent society that would not be a caricature of something else. It must contain conditions for people to make decisions; it must be a society that learns from experience — which a repressive, authoritarian society can never do."

Third world critics of conventional development strategies have also seen positive signs. Lokayan members, for example, point out that there are commmunities in the Indian state of Karnataka where the people have used traditional forms of government, known as

The Chipko (tree-hugging) movement began as a women's movement in the Himalayas and has inspired many similar groups throughout India.

Photo: Rod Berriedale Johnson

panchayats, to plan their local economies, and to reject large-scale development projects and rediscover old wells and ponds. In arid Rajasthan, Sunderal Bahaguna of the Chipko movement has been successful in persuading farmers to retain their water for their own use rather than sell it to industry. The growth of the Chipko movement is itself a positive sign. Beginning as a women's movement based in the Himalayas, it now has thousands of counterparts throughout the country.

Common to all these movements is a strong belief in the value of networking with one another for survival and regeneration from the ravages of so-called development. They value highly-localised water-management schemes, including check dams and storage ponds. They encourage tree conservation and planting, preferably although not necessarily of indigenous varieties, organic farming, and the use of biogas as energy.

Nor are such methods confined to India. We have already seen examples of such strategies in action in Malaysia (see Case Study 2) and similar examples can be found in Africa. In Kenya, for example, the Green Belt Movement encourages women and children to plant trees for use as fuelwood and to prevent soil erosion. Efforts are being made by ANEN, the Africa-wide environment and development co-ordination organisation based in Nairobi, to encourage people to use more fuel-efficient stoves for cooking as well as undertaking tree-planting and making use of seeds developed locally. And in neighbouring Tanzania peasant farmers have taken matters into their own hands by poisoning their coffee trees in defiance of the law, uprooting the dead trees and planting food for their own needs, because the price of coffee is so low.

The contrasting views of those seeking to implement the conventional wisdom of development and those who regard such actions as anti-developmental are well summarised in *Forestry Crisis and*

Box 4: The forest resource: two viewpoints

Shiva asks four questions, and finds that the answers she arrives at are totally at variance with the "official" view.

1. *Who destroys the forests?* The official view, according to Shiva, is that people are the cause of forest destruction. By contrast, she argues on behalf of the World Rainforest Movement that it is profit which destroys them.

2. *Who is a tropical forest expert?* The view as expressed in the World Resources Institute's report, *Tropical Forests: A Call for Action*, is that scientific knowledge of tropical forestry lies only with the experts in the aid-donor countries of the industrialised world. This view is rejected by Shiva, who argues that foreign experts are trained only in partisan forestry science which caters for markets and works against people and nature. The true tropical forest experts are women, peasants and forest dwellers because of their "on the ground" experience of the forests' environmental conditions.

3. *What is the most effective means of solving the biomass crisis of the poor?* *Tropical Forests* is of the opinion that it is only via the privatisation of resources that the poor will be provided with biomass efficiently. Shiva rejects this totally. She believes that privatisation has the opposite effect as it erodes the access and entitlement of the poorest people to both biomass and land.

4. *What is the most effective mechanism for ecological recovery?* The view expressed in the report is that profitability can be an exclusive and effective guide to ecological rehabilitation. This simply does not tally with the experience of Shiva and the World Rainforest Movement. They argue that forestation programmes which are based on profitability alone can become ecological hazards themselves, while an exclusive concern with profitability in the past has caused ecological destruction. This leads Shiva to conclude that a programme with an overriding concern for profitability is incapable of reversing ecological destruction.

Forestry Myths by Vandana Shiva (1987). In this booklet Shiva critically reviewed *Tropical Forests: A Call for Action* (1985), the joint report of the World Bank, the United Nations Development Programme (UNDP), and the World Resources Institute. On behalf of the Malaysian-based World Rainforest Movement, she concluded that its proposals would result in yet more ecocide. A summary of the radically differing views of the causes of and solutions to the destruction of the rainforests is contained in Box 4.

Shiva explicitly endorses the signs of hope identified by groups such as Lokayan and the Chipko movement. Clearly if women, peasants and forest dwellers are the true experts in tropical forest management, it is their action which will ensure that the forests are used in a sustainable fashion for their own and, ultimately, their countries' benefit. Shiva and the World Rainforest Movement are not opposed to the forests being used in profitable ways. Indeed, they argue that such groups of people have used the forests profitably from the start. However, there is a clear difference in the interpretation of "profit". For organisations such as Lokayan and the Chipko and World Rainforest Movements, profit means far more than financial gain; it includes such long-term notions as the sustainability of environmental use, protection of the ecosystem, and never taking more than can be replaced. They wish to ensure that it is not only their own generation, but also that of their children, which will benefit from conservation of the environment.

Further encouragement can be found in the success which groups like these have had in developing a new urgency amongst government planners. In the light of new evidence in New Delhi, for instance, officials have dramatically reconsidered their earlier view that care for the environment was a luxury which developing countries could not afford, or a device to deny poor countries the opportunity of catching up with the rich world. Increasingly, they are coming to the conclusion that environmental degradation is a cause of the drastic impoverishment of the already extremely poor. According to the second *Citizen's Report on the Environment* produced by the Centre for Science and the Environment, the average Indian now has only a quarter of the agricultural land which was available at independence, 40 years ago.

Not all governments have yet been convinced by the arguments advanced by the popular-based movements which question development policy based on conventional wisdom. As we have seen, the Indonesian government, for example, fully accepts the "official" view that people are the cause of environmental destruction. Nonetheless, a growing number of governments are recognising that although people will obviously have an impact on the environment — and have always done so — it is their poverty which causes them to act in an environmentally destructive manner.

Equally importantly, they are also coming to recognise that more often than not the *major* cause of environmental degradation is not poverty but short-sightedness or, worse, greed on the part of the commercial exploiters. It is clearly one or the other which determines company policies demanding the immediate maximisation of profit rather than taking a longer-term view. Similarly, one can legitimately argue that it is one or the other which permits the adoption of policies which were already known to have disastrous environmental results, such as the destruction of genetic reserves and species, with whose existence "modern" humanity was, and is, not fully cognisant.

A "new" economic theory
What then can be done? For Khor Kok Peng and the Consumers' Association of Penang, Malaysia, the answer is obvious — as it is for organisations such as Lokayan and the Chipko Movement. Khor Kok Peng believes that traditional economic policy design ignores the definitive role which what he terms the "People's Economy" should have. Traditional economics considers the public and private sectors; it is apparently unable to define the role of what economic traditionalists call the informal economy.

For Khor Kok Peng, the term itself is a misnomer which guarantees official hostility to activities in this area. He argues that the people active in the informal economy are not only those in urban areas who are traditionally viewed as being in the informal sector — street traders, rag pickers, or people doing odd jobs — but all those who make use of their own resources and their family's labour to make a living. Therefore, in his view, this sector includes farmers growing food and other crops for their own use and for sale; the small manufacturer or household craftsman making baskets, mats, clothes and household utensils; the hawker providing food; the carpenter building houses or making furniture; and, also, the homeless and squatters making their own homes, as well as the groups traditionally defined as falling within the informal sector. The two may well overlap in some areas, but the traditional definition is too limited.

Khor Kok Peng argues that governments have ignored the "People's Economy" to their cost, both in their development strategies and, even more importantly, in the strategies adopted to counteract the effects of economic recession. Were they to recognise that these people form a positive force for the development of a country, the beneficial effects could be enormous. Such a change of attitude would ensure the more productive use of resources which, under conventional policy, are often left lying idle or are wasted.

Thus, the granting of land rights to landless people squatting on land claimed by large companies, which are unable or unwilling to make use of it because of a lack of resources or the expectation of an increase in its value over time, would ensure that such groups would not only produce more but also that they would be prepared to display greater care for the land. Similarly, were governments to provide the means for small-scale producers — family-based traders, craftsmen, or small industries — to function legitimately by granting licences, channelling credit or providing services such as the necessary physical infrastructure (which may include sites to which the public have easy access), marketing, design, and management training, the potential benefits for the people and country would be huge. Khor Kok Peng states that: "since the formal economy cannot provide enough jobs, it should at least not hinder the people's own initiatives by refusing to free the resources required by the People's Economy".

Were this approach to be adopted, Khor Kok Peng believes that third world countries, including those such as Malaysia which aid donors regard as success stories, would have securely established the necessary conditions for their own true development. And there are sound and strictly technical reasons for believing that this analysis is well-founded. A government which followed such a policy would guarantee an immediate and more sustainable increase in wealth for the majority of its people and this increase would be based on the provision of goods and services for the domestic market.

As the wealth of the population increased, experience suggests that their personal savings would do so as well. These, together with the increased taxation revenue which government would receive, would enable higher levels of investment in the economy than is the case at present. Nor does such a strategy imply that the country should attempt to disengage from international trade. Indeed, such trade would obviously continue, but it would be based to a far greater extent on the surplus of goods produced rather than maximising the production of a limited number of goods or commodities at the expense of other, equally cost-efficient commodities, such as food or basic services (those described by Khor Kok Peng as falling within the "People's Economy").

There appears to be little here to contradict the nineteenth-century economic theory of comparative advantage developed by David Ricardo. If comparative advantage were not applicable, foreign suppliers would be active in the "People's Economy", meeting the demand for goods and services. The fact that they are not is only to be explained by their inability to compete with local people already active in this area. One can thus argue that conventional development theory and practice run counter to the earlier trade theory which they claim to promote.

Conclusion

In summary, the foregoing has surveyed mainstream development theory and practice as promoted by the most important development institution operating in the world today, namely, the World Bank. The Bank fills this role for a number of reasons. Firstly, it is usually the largest single aid donor. Furthermore, all the major Western bilateral donors are executive directors of the Bank, and are required to agree on Bank-supported projects. Hence one must assume that the governments which they represent, and who are the major shareholders in the World Bank, agree with the theory underpinning Bank development policy. Thirdly, bilateral donors generally follow the lead of the World Bank and are unlikely to support a development programme, whose funding has been refused by the World Bank. There are exceptions to this, of course, but more often than not they arise from domestic, political or trade concerns and, as such, may be said to prove the general rule.

Furthermore, we have shown that conventional development theory has remained constant throughout the three UN Development Decades reviewed. The basic premises which underpinned modernisation theory were carried forward and remain at the core of integration theory, as the present-day emphasis on economic growth through increased production for the export market shows. Even the most cursory examination of the structural adjustment programmes adopted by so many countries affected by the international debt crisis clearly demonstrates this. And it is argued by both the IMF and the World Bank that the reason why the debt crisis does not pose a serious problem for many major East Asian countries is, *inter alia*, because they have successfully followed the recommended path of export-led growth.

We have also seen that the implementation of conventional development theory has proved wanting in a number of ways. Foremost among these is its questionable economic effect. While economic advances have occurred, these have not been sufficient to improve the quality of life of all third world people. In fact, as the examples cited above indicate, the practice of development to date has frequently resulted in worsening conditions for the poor. In India, for example, the Green Revolution has led to increased levels of agricultural production and national food security; but the concomitant increase in irrigation has led to a falling water table, more intensive exploitation of the soil, frequently increased salinisation of the soil, and so on. The net result has been some short-term improvements with, very often, serious long-term effects. This argument has been accepted by the major development institutions and is, as we have seen, underlined by the publication of environmental guidelines by both the World Bank and, more recently, Britain's Overseas Development Administration.

Secondly, the emphasis on an all-out drive for economic growth through increased levels of production has had serious cultural repercussions. The opposition displayed by indigenous peoples in India and Malaysia to the construction of large dams and the logging of tropical forests respectively, stems as much from the threats posed to their way of life by such practices as it does from the loss of lands which have traditionally been regarded as theirs. Economic growth alone has clearly been inadequate to meet the needs of these groups of people for a combination of reasons, including inadequate conceptualisation and internal political conditions.

Environmentalist critiques of the development practice of the World

Bank and other donors have also been summarised. As epitomised by Jonathan Porritt and Michael Redclift, these argue that Bank-advocated policies are bound to fail because of the position held by third world countries in the international economic hierarchy. If all the peoples of the world were to consume its resources at the rate of the average North American or Western European, those resources would be depleted or so polluted as to be unusable within two, or at most three, generations. Furthermore, the essentially rational, if short-term, nature of the practices of private sector investors, particularly the transnational corporations, has been illustrated. Lastly, the critique argues that the debt crisis under which many developing countries laboured throughout the 1980s was directly attributable to the economic development model advocated by the IMF, the World Bank, and bilateral aid donors. These points result in Redclift and Porrit concluding that it is only through a fundamental restructuring of the international economy that development, which is sustainable, egalitarian and caring for the environment, can occur.

However, the Redclift and Porritt analysis has been found wanting, in that it fails adequately to address questions of domestic and international power relationships and interests. Furthermore, it fails to deal with the fundamental questions relating to trade and appears to advocate a static world view which, it has been argued, will be unable to meet the legitimate demands of the world's people for a decent quality of life.

We have surveyed in some detail, therefore, the exterior of the development umbrella. It is now time to go underneath the umbrella, in order to look at development from the perspective of those who experience it in practice.

Notes

11. Redclift and Porritt believe that the development and implementation of policies to attain wider goals than these require "radically-changed structural policies".

12. See *Just Food*, CAFOD, 1984.

13. It is important to acknowledge that Porritt rejects this charge outright. In *Seeing Green: The Politics of Ecology Explained*, Blackwell (Oxford, 1987) he asserts that a zero-growth position is absurd, and that "there will always continue to be some economic growth", while "in the Third World, there will have to be substantial ecomonic growth for some time". However, there is a world of difference between this assertion and what seems implicit in his and Redclift's analysis of the international economy.

CASE STUDY THREE
INTEGRATED DEVELOPMENT IN ERITREA

Photo: Stephen King/CAFOD

Ploughing with camel, Eritrea. The Mogaraib-Forto project aims to combine successful development with sustainable environmental care.

The Mogoraib-Forto integrated development project, which is financially assisted by CAFOD, has been deliberately selected as an example of what can be achieved in sustainable development terms, chiefly because of the project's size and scope. Many other projects assisted by CAFOD have substantial environmental care aspects in their make-up. For example, CAFOD-supported rehabilitation and development programmes have stressed the importance of utilising local seed-types rather than imported hybrid seeds, where this is most appropriate. Similarly, water and soil conservation has formed an important part of many of the CAFOD-assisted agricultural projects. However, these are on a far smaller scale. There is little dispute concerning the possibility of maximising popular participation in and ownership of such small-scale projects by local people. What is important is to demonstrate that this is possible on a far larger scale than that usual for non-governmental development organisations.

Eritrea, the contested province in northern Ethiopia, is bordered by Djibouti to the south-east, Sudan to the west, and the Red Sea to the east. Ethiopia rules the territory directly from the capital Addis Ababa, in breach of the United Nations agreement which established a federation of Ethiopia and Eritrea against the wishes of a substantial number of Eritreans in 1952. The Ethiopian government's subsequent assumption of direct rule was accompanied by the looting of the territory's economy; several industries, for example, were dismantled and removed to Addis Ababa, and an attempt was made to suppress the local culture through, *inter alia*, ending the teaching of the Eritrean languages, Tigrinya and Tigre, and the repeal of local rights and powers of institutions. Strikes by workers against the rapidly-rising unemployment which resulted, and boycotts and demonstrations by school students, were brutally suppressed, leaving several hundred opponents of Ethiopian rule dead and wounded.

These events, far from ending opposition to Ethiopian rule, only served to formalise it. In 1961, opposition groups drawn from traditional leaders formed the Eritrean Liberation Front (ELF) to promote armed resistance to the Ethiopians. In 1970, a breakaway group split from the ELF, citing its failure to change traditional hierarchical social structures, and formed the Eritrean People's Liberation Front (EPLF). The ELF's strength and influence were further dissipated by a series of factional disputes so that the EPLF today represents the majority of Eritreans opposed to Ethiopian rule and is the only significant anti-Ethiopian military presence in the territory. Effectively there has been a state of war since 1961 but armed resistance increased substantially following the formation of the EPLF. Hopes prompted by the overthrow of Haile Selassie in 1974 proved groundless and the conflict has been considerably stepped up since 1976.

It is a war which experience suggests neither side can win militarily, while the real losers are the inhabitants of the area over which it is being fought. Thousands of Eritreans have fled, seeking refuge in neighbouring Sudan or in the rural areas of the territory controlled by the EPLF. The Eritrean Relief Association (ERA) was established to meet the relief and development needs of these people, and to help them become self-sufficient again.

CAFOD's involvement grew out of its experience of ERA's success in ensuring that the refugees and displaced people received emergency relief during the height of the famine which devastated much of sub-Saharan Africa during 1984-86. This experience of partnership was further developed through ERA's promotion of such rehabilitation and development programmes as were possible in a war situation. At present, CAFOD's major involvement is the funding of the substantial Mogoraib-Forto Comprehensive Development Project.

Intended to benefit the 23,000 inhabitants of the south central region of Barka province, the project was devised by ERA in close consultation with the people of the area. This has ensured, in so far as is humanly possible, that all aspects of an integrated development strategy have been included in the planning of the programme. Thus, existing links between farming, irrigation, soil and water conservation, reforestation, health, social services such as education, and transport and communications have been identified and developed under the plan into a coherent whole.

Important parts of the agricultural component are:
● the provision of tools for the area's 3,000 farmers, and forges so that more tools can be manufactured locally;
● the provision of large sheets of iron and harnesses to be used by farmers in levelling and terracing their land, for which they will be paid. In all, 6,230 hectares of crop land will be terraced by human- and ox-power and provided with the necessary earth embankments to stop erosion. The area's farmers have taken this up with such enthusiasm that work on 26 of the 29 sites identified for the whole five-year period had already started by the end of 1988, and was completed on 14 sites;
● the purchase of seeds either in local markets or in neighbouring Sudan, in order to make sure that they are the most appropriate to local conditions. The poor 1987 harvest meant that the seeds distributed in 1988 had to be bought in Sudan but, in the Mogaraib area at least, farmers stressed their preference for local seeds and chose to exchange or eat the distributed (and better-tasting) seed so that they could plant traditional Wadferge sorghum seed;
● encouraging vegetable gardening on suitable soils, irrigating the gardens with water drawn by pumps from hand-dug wells, two of which are planned to overcome the danger of an excessive depletion of groundwater. Supply problems, due to the heavy rains which the area experienced during mid-1988, delayed the delivery of the pumps. Furthermore, it is planned to maximise the irrigation possibilities of the area's three rivers and their tributaries by the construction of diversion canals so as to flood neighbouring fields. Considerable work on this aspect was carried out during 1988 and the farmers have shown a clear commitment to future project planning by their

suggestion that the canal banks should be protected from erosion by wire mesh and stones rather than the more expensive concrete initially envisaged;
● the establishment of two tree-nurseries for demonstration purposes, so that eventually 120 hectares can be reforested with local species of trees. In all, it is hoped that about 2,700 farmers will become involved in the reforestation programme. However, the farmers showed considerable reluctance during 1988 to commit the necessary amount of time to care for the seedlings. Only one small trial plot was established during the year, and although the trees on this plot have grown to a height of between 3 and 4 metres, it required the full-time employment of three people with donkeys to water the seedlings;
● veterinary services, which are an important element providing protection against diseases not only for the stock already in the area but also the oxen which are needed for work to combat erosion through terracing.

The second major component of the project is the provision of clean water and the improvement of communications. Thus, in addition to the two wells for irrigation purposes mentioned above, 15 wells for drinking water were planned for construction during the five years of the programme. Construction of the wells, both for drinking and irrigation purposes, has been delayed by the war situation and the need to refurbish water supplies in the towns evacuated by the Ethiopian forces in April

Photo: Mike Goldwater/NETWORK

Pastoralists learning from the ERA how to farm land irrigated by well water in the plane of the River Barka.

and May, 1988. The construction of two road networks, totalling 56 kilometres in all, is meant to enable the farmers' increased production to be efficiently marketed. Maintenance will be undertaken by the communities benefiting from their construction. By the end of the year ERA reported that 21 kilometres of road had been completed. This was regarded as a considerable success because the start of work had been delayed by the need to camouflage the equipment.

Health care provision is the third component. Most of the diseases affecting the population of the area are easily preventable and curable. Ensuring a supply of clean water will go some way in this. Two local health centres for primary health care and education, staffed by two health assistants and aided by 12 trained barefoot doctors, were in operation after a year, but still in temporary structures. ERA hopes to build more permanent structures once the security situation has stabilised.

Education is clearly a priority in the region, which is known to have a serious illiteracy problem. Four schools are planned with double teaching shifts where necessary, but, once again, the uncertain security situation has caused a revision of plans and only two schools were opened in 1988.

The final component is the provision of social services. As a start in the attempt to reduce the workload of women, two flour mills, with a total milling capacity of 24,000 quintals (approximately 2,400 tonnes), are planned.

ERA is responsible for financial accounting and reporting on the project. Popular participation in the programme is promoted and ensured by trained project facilitators living in the villages and working closely with existing village organisations. The enthusiasm already shown by the farmers for terracing their land and harnessing flood waters for irrigation purposes is a consequence of the local people's perception of the benefits which will accrue to them as a result of the programme and the extent to which they feel they own the project. ERA has made great efforts through extensive consultation during the planning process to ensure that these conditions are met, although it has clearly been more successful in some aspects of the programme than in others. It is hoped that the successful implementation of all the components will encourage the maintenance of popular enthusiasm.

The programme is, therefore, a clear example of popular participation. But it is also intended to meet the requirement, suggested as a norm by Manfred Maxneef, that it should create the conditions for its replication. Thus, care for the area's eco-system is a vital part. The reforestation portion of the programme, for example, has a threefold aim — soil conservation, the provision of fuel and fodder for stock, and the replenishment of local tree species. However, as the farmers were reluctant to devote the necessary time to its successful implementation, ERA has suggested that in the short term they should build terraces around the upper parts of their fields in order to deter erosion and encourage the natural vegetation to recover. The longer-term importance of reforestation has not been discounted. Suggestions of how to encourage greater enthusiasm amongst farmers include food-for-work programmes and demonstrating the value of trees as animal fodder.

Similarly, it is hoped that plans to conserve soil and water through terracing and the construction of canals to divert water for spate (flood) irrigation of crops, which have been partly responsible for harvests of up to 20 quintals (2 tonnes) per hectare in 1988, will guarantee the land's future fertility and ensure adequate water supplies. Also important were the decisions to dig only a limited number of wells in order to conserve groundwater, and to rely on seeds purchased in local or Sudanese markets.

The design of the other components of the programme is also intended to maximise the potential for sustainability. Thus, it is hoped that improved health and education standards will both enable the people to work harder for their own benefit and also reduce the incentive to have very large families. Higher incomes from increased production and better marketing should provide the local people with more disposable cash to buy the goods they need. These may be manufactured locally — the supply of two forges should remove one of the blockages on the manufacture of farm implements — or, the war permitting, will be able to be brought into the area more easily via the new roads.

The war was largely responsible for creating the conditions which made the programme necessary in the first place, and it will continue to be the major influence on the programme's future prospects. Military action in the area would destroy overnight many months, or even years, of effort by ERA and the local people. Ultimately, the project's success is dependent on a resolution of the conflict between the Ethiopian Government and the EPLF. Nonetheless, the enthusiasm and determination of the people of the area to improve their quality of life, coupled with ERA's proven expertise in planning and implementing successful development programmes in partnership with local people, provide grounds for optimism.

CHAPTER 5

SOME CRITICAL ENVIRONMENTAL ISSUES IN DEVELOPMENT

Any attempt to investigate popular experience of development in the Third World must try to identify what the people involved regard as critical environmental issues. Failure to do this is likely to result in a review so brief and generalised as to be meaningless. Furthermore, the wider the angle of focus, the less likely it is that one will be able to identify popularly-based alternatives to mainstream practice, both in terms of resistance and locally identified development needs.

Many people in developing countries agree with the underlying principle of conventional development theory — that development is needed to improve the quality of life for all. As we have already seen, their interpretation of how best to achieve this varies. For some, particularly members of ruling elites, conventional methods are best. One of the difficulties which aid donors have experienced in implementing policies reflecting environmental concern has stemmed from the perception of some third world governments that environmental concerns are luxuries which their countries cannot afford. Until recently the Indian federal government subscribed to such a view, and, in the light of evidence provided by the Narmada Valley Development Scheme and the Suvernarekha Irrigation System (see Case Study 1), some state governments in India apparently still do.

Regardless of where they live, ordinary people generally do not use words like "environment" or "development". By and large, they tend to leave such labels to so-called experts, preferring to concentrate on everyday things such as how much litter there is outside their houses; whether the water they use is clean; whether they are able to catch enough fish, or reap an adequate crop to meet their needs; and whether their descendants will also be able to do these things. Ordinary people, in other words, have a very different perspective on development and the environment in which they live from that which occupies the attention of theorists. In the words of one CAFOD partner talking about the Gabbra people of northern Kenya, "they do not have a concept of the environment which is separate".

Thus, in order to view the underside of the development umbrella, one has to try and see how people in developing countries perceive their everyday reality, identify what they regard as the most important issues facing them, and see how they have tried to meet the challenges which these have posed. Highlighting these concerns will permit us to consider the effects on the environment of the conflict of interests between different groups in a society. It will also allow us to test the contention that much of the development experience has a fundamentally different concept of expertise — the expertise of the people versus the intellectual expertise of development planners — at its root.

Four broad headings would appear to encompass such popular concerns within the overall theoretical context identified: land, particularly its degradation; water, and the use to which it is put; the rights of the inhabitants of an area, particularly those of indigenous

Water, carried up to the fields by human chain, is directed down different channels in turn to irrigate vegetables (Nafka, Eritrea). Water availability is often a crucial factor in successful development.

Photo: Mike Goldwater/NETWORK

people; and the exploitation of resources. There are obviously points at which these overlap but these reinforce the importance of the general themes of discussion. We will now consider each of these in turn, seeking to identify why it is critical.

Increasing land degradation

As we have already noted, the earth's land surface is under increasing attack. Careless use of tropical forests alone destroys 11 million hectares of forest a year. Cattle ranching schemes, such as those in Brazil's Amazon region (see description in *Land and Poverty*, 1987) have underlined the fragility of tropical soils which depend on the forest for constant replenishment. Removing the forest cover destroys the soil's fertility. Passengers in aircraft flying over the Brazilian Amazon region can see plumes of smoke and vast scars across the forest, testimony to the destruction wreaked by loggers, miners and settlers pushing back one of the last frontiers in the world today.

Tropical areas are not the only parts of the world's land surface under threat. As the Brundtland Report observes, 6 million hectares of grassland, much of it on the African continent, succumbs to the process of desertification annually. For most people this conjures up images of an inexorable southward movement of the Sahara desert. But in fact, the process of desertification resembles rather a "bad skin disease, outbreaks of which appear whenever people have exhausted their land by overworking it; the individual patches then join together, leading to the day when the entire body will be affected" (see Nigel Twose, *Fighting the Famine*, 1985, a report on the Sahel region of sub-Saharan Africa, jointly commissioned by CAFOD). Before going on to identify some of the methods which the people have adopted to counteract the loss of productive land, we need first to ask why they are prepared to jeopardise their long-term future by overworking it in the first place.

It should to be noted at the outset that the land's exhaustion does not stem either from natural causes (drought) or from the ignorance of people living in the area. In Africa's Sahel region (which stretches south of the Sahara desert, from the continent's west coast to the east coast state of Somalia) a delicate balance between pastoral and settled agriculture has been maintained for centuries. Traditionally, pastoralists grazed their thinly-spread herds on the marginal land close to the desert's edge, moving closer to settled agricultural areas after the crops had been harvested. During the dry winter months their herds grazed in the harvested fields, replenishing the land's fertility, and the farmers exchanged part of their harvest and the use of their fields by the pastoralists' animals for milk and, occasionally, meat. When the rains were about to resume, the pastoralists returned to their summer grazing grounds, leaving the farmers to plough and replant their fields, which had been fertilised during the winter months.

The system, as it emerged over time, was clearly not as ideal as might be thought from the above description. The method of social

Photo: Liba Taylor/CAFOD

A pastoralist at a well in northern Somalia, Sahel region.

organisation was also imperfect; conflicts of interest, possibly resulting in violence, undoubtedly occurred between the nomads and the settled farmers. And both populations experienced all the hardships associated with life under difficult conditions. However, the fact that this means of social organisation survived for so long clearly underlines the value it had for both the nomads and the settled farmers. At least as important a reason for its survival was its maintenance of a careful ecological balance — for without this, there would have been no possibility of human life in the area. It was dependent on three main factors: a mutually satisfactory interaction between the two groups, water availability and an appropriate land to population ratio. Had any of these been absent, ecological imbalance — and ultimately collapse — would have resulted.

i. *Mutually satisfactory interaction.* As the system worked, both the settled farmers and the pastoralists benefited, at least most of the time. Had either party been dissatisfied with the exchange, it would not have continued. Had the farmers been dissatisfied, they would have either demanded more or provided the pastoralists with less. Had the pastoralists felt that the farmers' demands were exorbitant, they would have sought others with whom to trade.

ii. *Water availability.* This was clearly crucial, although not in the way that might have been expected. Too great a supply of water in any one place would clearly have disrupted the migratory patterns of the pastoralists. For example, had substantial water supplies been available in the immediate environs of the area settled by the farmers, the pastoralists would have been discouraged from moving away during the summer months. This would have disrupted the cycle and resulted in overgrazing, as has occurred since the sinking of wells following the severe drought which affected the area in the late 1960s and early 1970s. The availability of water also affects the size of herds; because of cultural norms in pastoralist societies where the size of a herd reflects the wealth of its owners, the existence of water supplies encourages pastoralists to increase their herds in line with the availability of water. Thus, too great or too concentrated a supply of water can have an environmentally damaging effect as herd sizes increase, leading to overgrazing and destruction of the land.

iii. *Land to population ratio*. To a certain extent, this issue has already been touched upon. Substantial increases in herd size clearly disrupt the balance established, as the experience of the past 15 years has shown. Pastoralists, responding to the incentives provided by governments and aid agencies who ensured that additional water supplies were available, have increased the size of their herds and settled around the wells. This results in significant overgrazing of the area and the southward spread of the desert.

Much the same pattern applies to the number of people living permanently in one area. As numbers increase, the availability of land decreases, permitting fewer fallow periods. Forced by necessity to keep land in production, farmers either have to apply more fertilisers or accept the overworking of their land, and its eventual loss of fertility and degradation. Furthermore, increased population increases the demand for fuel; wider and wider swathes of land around the settlements are subject to deforestation which both takes up more time (women have to go further afield to collect firewood, and consequently have less time for farming) and increases the land's vulnerability to erosion and eventual desertification.

The intervention of well-intentioned development projects into this situation disrupted the balance which had been established over centuries. Following the Sahelian drought between 1968 and 1973, aid programmes in the region sought to protect the area's people from future drought in two ways. Firstly, water supplies were increased; thousands of wells were sunk providing irrigation for export and food crops and drinking water for people and animals. Secondly, the people were encouraged to enter the cash economy; farmers were encouraged to produce crops for export and pastoralists to improve and increase the size of their herds.

The extent of aid was considerable. Lloyd Timberlake (*Africa in Crisis*, Earthscan, 1985) states that between 1974 and 1981 aid to the Sahelian countries increased substantially, rising from US $756 million in 1974 to US$1,970 million in 1981. Its purpose was agreed by both donors and the Sahel's governments — "to establish food self-sufficiency in the region". However, this failed to occur in practice. Approximately 35% of all aid to the region consisted of food aid of various types to help with balance of payments difficulties and to

87

various Sahelian organisations. Another third was spent on infrastructural projects, including transport, telecommunications, health, education and water supplies. The remainder was allocated to projects defined as "productive in principle" such as irrigated and rain-fed agriculture. By far the vast majority of this directly-productive aid, however, went to export-oriented agriculture. Only 4% was spent on rain-fed food crops while 1.5% was spent on projects (such as tree planting and soil and water conservation) which sought to rehabilitate and protect the environment, and which were necessary to improve the resource base on which rain-fed agriculture depends.

During the early years, the aid appeared to achieve remarkable success. The provision of water was accompanied by the expansion of health services which encouraged pastoralists to settle more permanently. Furthermore, supplies of water encouraged farmers to cultivate land which had previously had received inadequate amounts of rainfall (less than 300 mm a year). For a while, it appeared as if the goal of securing the future of the people of the region was in sight. But it was not to be. The settlement of pastoralists and their herds around water supplies resulted in overgrazing on such a scale that the land had little chance to recover. In addition, the few trees in the area of the settlements were soon cut down, speeding up erosion and environmental destruction. Finally, the increasing numbers of settled farmers in an area unsuited to agricultural exploitation hastened the process of erosion and environmental degradation.

Some environmentalists believe that the process has gone so far as to be irreversible. They point out that the destruction of ground cover in the form of trees, grass and shrubs can result in long-term climatic

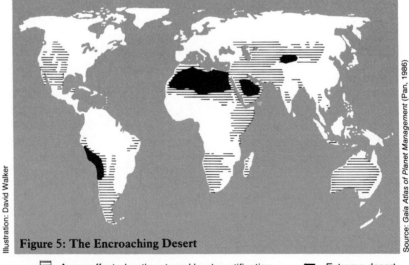

Illustration: David Walker

Source: *Gaia Atlas of Planet Management* (Pan, 1986)

Figure 5: The Encroaching Desert

☰ Areas affected or threatened by desertification   ■ Extreme desert changes. More heat is reflected by a bare surface than by one which is covered, resulting in higher air temperatures, less condensation, and hence lower rainfall. Such lower rainfall levels further reinforce the process as there is less moisture to enable the land to recover. In addition, the rain which does fall seldom seeps into the hardened, sun-baked earth; more often it hastens the process of erosion sweeping the remaining topsoil away, a process which is exacerbated by wind.

Viewed from the present day, the actions of people in the Sahel region during the recent past may appear illogical. But, as has been shown, they had good reasons for acting as they did. The intervention of well-meaning foreign aid donors in the area led to an increase in the supply of water, with two results. On the one hand, small farmers who were experiencing a shortage of land began farming in more marginal areas which had formerly been part of the pastoralists' grazing lands. On the other, the pastoralists, having access to more water for their herds, increased their herd sizes. This placed still further pressure on the land. In the long term, these two developments alone would probably have been enough to cause the degradation described above. But the encouragement which the pastoralists, in particular, received to settle through the provision of services, such as health care and education, speeded up the process of degradation and dramatically increased both communities' vulnerability to the next cycle of bad weather. Few people, if any, would argue that any single measure advocated and financed by the aid donors was wrong. But their combination had disastrous results for the people of the Sahel and underlined the donors' failure to understand that the results of their intervention would spread far beyond the confines of economic theory.

Reversing the process
i. *Individually.* African people and governments, however, have refused to accept such despairing fatalism, which predicts the irreversibility of the area's environmental degradation. In many parts of the continent, people have come together in an effort to reverse the process. In Eritrea (as we saw in Case Study 3), large numbers are engaged in the construction of earth dams to conserve water, for, as Timberlake notes, Africa needs thousands more dams which are of a manageable size, rather than the emphasis on huge dams beloved of governments and aid donors. Similar CAFOD-assisted programmes are under way in many Sahel countries in West Africa, as well as in northern Kenya. Soil conservation projects, involving terracing and encouraging tree-planting, are also under way throughout the continent.

One of the few popularly-based reforestation programmes on a national scale is the Kenyan Green Belt Movement, organised by the National Council of Women of Kenya (NCWK). The project has three main objectives. Firstly, it promotes an understanding of the relationship between the environment and other issues such as food production and health. In this, education is critical. Children gain exposure through green belt projects at their schools; small farmers learn to appreciate the connections between forestry, soil conservation, and their own needs for wood. Secondly, the project aims to integrate the physically disabled population and young school-leavers into their communities, thereby increasing their prospects of remaining in the communities rather than migrating to urban areas in search of jobs or charity. These groups are encouraged to look after the newly-planted trees on behalf of the whole community. Finally, the project seeks to promote a positive image of women. Women are involved as equal participants in the development of green belts. The training which they receive in the planting and cultivation of seedlings provides another source of female income. And the establishment of green belts has done much to reduce the time which they have to spend gathering fuelwood over increasingly large areas.

The Green Belt Movement distributes seedlings free to those expressing an interest in the programme. But first the interested individual or group has to prepare the available land according to the movement's requirements. The future needs of the seedlings are also fully discussed so that participants understand their obligations. In this way, a high survival rate for the trees has been ensured. Follow-up is carried out by "Green Belt Rangers", who are often physically disabled members of the community whose job it is to check on the care and maintenance of the trees and offer advice.

The movement has achieved considerable success. Public awareness of environmental issues in Kenya has grown substantially — to such an extent that by late 1987 it was found necessary to establish a national environmental and development co-ordinating body in Nairobi. Some 65 community nurseries have been established as a result of the movement, which estimates that thousands of trees have been planted throughout the country.

ii. *Nationally*. Approximately 645 kilometres off Africa's west coast, Cape Verde is implementing a broadly similar programme with the help of both official aid organisations and NGOs. With finance from the EC, the major donor, USAID, and the FAO, some 17 million trees have been planted since independence in 1975. This is all the more remarkable because, to all intents and purposes, the country is an off-shore extension of the Sahara desert. Its average rainfall is 300 mm a year, all of which falls within approximately ten days in August; for the rest of the year the weather is hot, dry and windy. The trees were planted during the course of a 20-year long drought which only ended with good rains in 1987 — small wonder, then, that, as the prime minister's chief of staff put it: "When the rains start in August, we all leave the office and go out and plant. It's fun."

Ultimately, it is hoped to transform the dry, barren islands of the archipelago into lush, green oases. The forestry programme is vital to the process as the trees stop soil erosion, provide firewood and,

Photo: Diana East/Panos Pictures

Santiago Island, Cape Verde: a vast reforestation programme, where terracing and planting is carried out by government-funded workers.

eventually, modify the climate. But, as well as planting trees, the people are building dams, dykes, wells and watersheds in order to help stop the rain from rushing straight down the mountains and into the sea.

They know that they have a long way to go. Nonetheless, popular support for the programme is extensive. Approximately 10% of the country's surface is planted and the survival rate of the seedlings is high, at around 85%. This supports the observations made by aid workers that the Cape Verdians have understood that trees literally mean their survival. According to Martino Meloni, the EEC representative, "There is tremendous respect for trees here, even at the lowest levels of society. You will never see a person cutting down a tree. You will see them trimming carefully. To Cape Verdians, trees are like beautiful flowers."

What lessons, then, can be drawn from the foregoing discussion? Firstly, there are signs of hope coming from the continent. And perhaps the clearest is that the hope originates in the actions of the African people themselves either alone, as in the case of the Green Belt Movement, or in projects with outside help such as the CAFOD-assisted Mogoraib-Forto Integrated Development Project (Case Study 3) or the Cape Verde reforestation programme. Secondly, there is the recognition and further development of African people's expertise. Thirdly, there is the need to involve the community fully in any project or programme. All three examples cited above demonstrate such community involvement and a popular ownership of the schemes which augurs well for their continuing success.

Photo: ODA

The Victoria Dam, Sri Lanka. The construction of large dams often encourages the spread of water-borne diseases.

Water and its uses

The importance of the availability of water to the continuation of everyday life is generally recognised. What is seldom given the same priority is the use to which water is put. Many NGOs — CAFOD among them — have expressed deep reservations about large-scale irrigation projects which in many instances benefit the already wealthy and powerful rather than the poor, particularly in Asia and Latin America where land ownership patterns are grossly unequal. That this need not alway be the pattern is shown by a significant minority of cases — such as in the Indian state of Kerala, in South Korea during the late 1940s and 1950s, or in the People's Republic of China. However, if water for irrigation is to be available to those who need it most, then it is important that the authorities have a legislative framework in place to ensure this — and possess the political will to enforce it.

Further problems arise from the way water is stored for use. Many large-scale irrigation projects currently involve the construction of huge dams which in numerous instances have resulted in the spread of water-borne diseases, including the debilitating schistosomiasis (*bilharzia*) which is well documented in Africa. In parts of Egypt, for example, the completion of the Aswan Low Dam increased the levels of infestation of the local population from 21 to 75%, and to 100% in some communities following the completion of the High Dam. In Sudan, the implementation of the Gezira scheme, providing for the irrigation of 900,000 hectares of cotton, found a general infestation rate of between 60 and 70%, with higher rates for children — over 90% for school children.

Dams are not the only source of infestation. Irrigation schemes in

Kenya around Lake Victoria have resulted in almost all the school children in the relevant areas being infested. The creation of large, still bodies of water greatly facilitates the spread of the parasite. This is borne out by evidence from South Africa where it has been found that 68% of black farmworkers on well-irrigated white-owned farms are infested with the parasite in contrast with only 33% of blacks farming in the *bantustans*, where there is little irrigation.

But irrigation is only one of the uses to which water is put. Approximately three-quarters of the earth's surface is water, 97% of which is salt. The world's seas and oceans have been put to a variety of uses over time, probably the two most important being the harvesting of seafood and as a vast rubbish tip. Examples of both abound, but it is perhaps worthwhile to look in greater detail at an example from the Philippines, where industrial pollution has resulted in the destruction of the livelihood of local fishing communities. In this instance, too, the relative economic and political power of those involved has determined the way in which the water has been used.

Industrial pollution in the Philippines

The island of Marinduque is located roughly in the centre of the Philippines archipelago, and is dominated by two main economic activities: mining (the most important employers being the Marcopper Mining Corporation and the Marinduque Mining and Industrial Corporation) and fishing. Marcopper was established in 1964 to exploit the copper deposits discovered on the western slope of Mount Tapian. The company is owned by the Philippine-based Performance Investment Corporation (48%); Placer Development Ltd, of Vancouver, Canada (40%); with the remaining 12% of shares owned by individual shareholders. The company is heavily in debt to foreign banks, the principal UK creditors being Barclays and Lloyds banks. In effect, the company has defaulted on its loans, having managed only partial payments (totalling US$2.5 million) of past interest payments due. According to the National Secretariat for Social Action (NASSA) of the Bishops' Conference of the Philippines, CAFOD's partner organisation in the country, a total of 1,156 regular and probationary employees was employed at the mine at the end of 1985.

The Marcopper company engages in open-cast copper mining and refines 9.2 million tons of copper concentrate a year. The refining process produces 750,000 dry metric tonnes of waste (tailings) a month. When mining started in 1969, the tailings were deposited on land in the San Antonio Tailings Pond, approximately three kilometres from the concentrator, but the discovery in 1975 of a high-grade ore body beneath the site of the pond led the management to discharge the tailings directly into Calancan Bay. By 1983, these deposits covered 38 sq km; five years later, NASSA estimated that this had increased to 50 sq km.

As NASSA observes, "some 14,000 fishermen and their families depend on the bay for their livelihood". It is important, therefore, to identify the effect the company's actions have had on the bay's ecosystem and the resulting effects on the quality of life enjoyed by the fishing communities. The bay's ecosystem was not unusual: mangroves were a typical component of the shoreline, eelgrass was predominant on the inner portions of the reef, while the exterior was covered by algae. All in all, over 40 species of macrobermic algae were observed to grow in the bay, together with sponges, coelenterates, annelids, anthropods, and a wide variety of fish. The fish life had been so plentiful that, in the early 1970s, an individual average catch after two hours weighed between 20 and 30 kilograms.

Conditions changed rapidly after 1975 when the discharge of mine tailings into the bay began. Within four years it was apparent that both the number and the population of species had fallen, and by the early 1980s the number of species in the algae community had declined by 60% and its frequency by 83%. The eelgrass community also showed a distinct decrease. The discharge of mine tailings reduced sunlight penetration, impaired nutrient efficiency, and increased the amount of mechanical and physical abrasion which causes the algae to deteriorate. The net effect of this ecological change was a decrease of fish and other marine life which depend on the algae for food.

As the reef's condition deteriorated, the coral community also declined. The destruction of the corals, which serve as fish food and shelter, has accelerated the decline of the fish population as they sought refuge in other locations. A fisheries survey of the bay has found that the density of volume of fish was considerably lower than in other areas.

This decline has had a substantial effect on the livelihoods of local fishermen. Overall, catches have declined by approximately 90% since 1975 and the incidence of malnutrition amongst children in the area is rising. Whereas small-scale commercial fishing was fairly common in the past, the whole community has now been forced back upon subsistence fishing. One local fisherman explains: "Before, we could fill our fishing boats with a variety of the choicest fishes. But now, we can hardly fill a coconut shell with fish and meagrely fill our stomachs for the day." The bay's pollution has also meant longer hours and greater costs for the fishermen as they have to go to sea much earlier than in the past, and travel further in search of unpolluted fishing grounds. Few can afford the added fuel costs.

The fishing communities are not the only ones to be affected. During the dry season strong winds carry inland fine particles of the tailings, which amass to form a virtual desert in the bay, and then deposits them on agricultural land, destroying plant life and contaminating the villagers' drinking water. The medical records of coastal residents show a higher incidence of respiratory and skin diseases than is common amongst people living in other parts of the island, with a particularly high incidence of respiratory illnesses during the summer.

Local residents also reported suffering severe stomach pains and diarrhoea after eating shellfish while these were still abundant. Cases of food poisoning after eating fish caught in the bay have also been reported. Children playing in the bay's water have frequently developed large sores on their legs and arms and some have developed rashes covering their bodies which lasted for several weeks. According to local people, none of these illnesses were experienced before the tailings were dumped in the bay.

Efforts by the local communities to stop Marcopper's dumping have been under way since 1978. They appeared to achieve limited success in 1981 when the National Pollution Control Commission (NPCC), the body responsible for making sure that companies operate in a manner which is not environmentally damaging, instructed the Marcopper to stop dumping in the bay. This instruction was overturned, however, by the then president, Ferdinand Marcos, who successfully pressured the NPCC to permit the company to resume the dumping of a reduced amount of tailings (7,000 metric tonnes). Marcos's interest in the issue was revealed by the disclosure by the Presidential Commission on Good Government established by his successor, Corazan Aquino, that he had owned Performance Investment Corporation's 48% holding in Marcopper.

The local people's hopes were raised by the overthrow of Marcos in February 1986. Assisted by Lingkod Tao-Kalikasan (Secretariat for an Ecologically Sound Philippines) and the local Church, each of the 12 barangays (villages) asked through their pastoral councils for the cessation of dumping in the bay and regeneration of marine life. Complaints were telegraphed to the president, the ministers of natural resources, agriculture and food, and to NPCC officials. With the help of Lingkod Tao-Kalikasan, contact has been maintained with pollution victims in the neighbouring areas of Santa Cruz and other parts of Marinduque, as well as with the NPCC and other environmental groups in the country and abroad.

This popular mobilisation proved initially successful. In September 1986, the NPCC instructed Marcopper to end all dumping in the bay immediately. The NPCC order stated that dumping would be allowed to resume only when the company had installed an NPCC-approved tailings disposal system. Furthermore, a technical committee comprising representatives of the NPCC, Marcopper, and the Bureau of Mines and Geo-Sciences was set up to find an alternative disposal system. Despite Marcopper's appeal against the conditional permission to renew operations in November 1986 which required it to resume using the San Antonio Pond, the president's office refused to intervene and overrule the Pollution Adjudication Board's findings. Regrettably, the president's office quickly changed its mind, and in mid-May 1987 issued a directive allowing the company to resume operations.

There are three possible explanations for this volte face. Firstly, as we have seen, the company is heavily in debt as is the Philippines itself. Both are in desperate need of foreign exchange to service their debts, and copper exports are needed in order to earn this. The government was engaged in negotiations to reschedule its foreign debt, of which the Marcopper debt forms a part, and the cessation of operations would hardly have been a positive influence on creditors engaged in these negotiations. Secondly, when the company ceased operating without any notice at midday on 19 April 1987 it cut off the island's electricity supply as well. (Marcopper had been supplying the province with electricity since 1985.) According to NASSA, Marcopper attempted to blame the local church authorities for the loss of electricity. The mayor of Santa Cruz, who had originally given the company permission to dump mine tailings in the bay in 1975 and who supplies the company with lime, organised a rally to protest at the interference in the company's operations by popular and church-supported environmental groups.

Thirdly, the company had announced plans to submerge its tailings pipe. Although the proposal fails to meet the standards laid down in 1981 by the NPCC (which require a depth of 60 metres, a strong current and a steep sea-bottom slope — none of which are possible or present in Calancan Bay), it is possible that this plan provided the excuse for the president's office to rescind its earlier decision not to interfere. However, according to Sister Aida Velasquez of Lingkod Tao-Kalikasan, the company's proposal will do nothing to halt the increase of pollution in the bay. In addition to wasting money on an ineffective tailings-disposal system she claims that: "If Marcopper...maintains the same direction of the discharge pipes, the mine tailings will soon cover [the bay] entirely and overrun the last piece of fishing ground of the fishermen which lies directly in their path."

Despite this setback the efforts of the local people to protect their environment have continued, with the support of NASSA. On 22 April 1988, Bishop Francisco Claver, NASSA's national director, issued a statement to this effect on behalf of NASSA's board.

It is valuable to tease out why these efforts managed to achieve what they did, and why they failed to achieve even more. The company clearly had, and retains, considerable influence with the Philippines government — which is not surprising, given that the latter guaranteed Marcopper's debt and assumed ownership of Marcos's 48% stake in the company on behalf of the country as a whole. Thus, the negotiations under way with the Philippines' creditors probably had a direct bearing on the president's decision to allow a resumption of operations. Furthermore, the company is influential in the island's political and economic life. The mayor benefits from his contract to supply lime and, therefore, has a direct interest in Marcopper's continued operation. So too do its employees and their dependants. And the company's role in supplying the island with electricity is likely to ensure support amongst residents for its continued operations. These factors explain why the mayor was able to show some popular support for a resumption of its activities after it ceased operations in April 1987.

By contrast, those who depend on fishing for their livelihood are more numerous and have the support of both the local church and of the environmental organisation, Lingkod Tao-Kalikasan. This means that the community has been able to make representations to the NPCC. The latter'sindependence has been demonstrated by the fact that both the 1981 order to Marcopper to cease operations and the November 1986 order permitting operations under certain conditions had to be overruled by the president. However, that they could be overruled, allowing the interests of a few to outweigh those of the majority of the community, is an indication of the NPCC's inherent weakness. Thus, the NASSA Board's public support for the majority of the people of Marinduque, following the 1988 pastoral letter, *The Cry of Our Land*, is important. It represents a further widening of the possible influence which can be brought to bear on the government to halt and reverse the progressive destruction of Calancan Bay.

Development and indigenous peoples' rights
Conflict between people and groups is not confined to third world societies, as any reading of the history of western European consolidation and expansion will show. Competition for power, influence and wealth formed the basis of these earlier conflicts, and similar conflicts, although not on the same scale, continue today. In many parts of the developing world, principally in Latin America and Asia, the more modern parts of society have come into conflict with so-called tribal peoples. At stake is the ownership of the many different forms of wealth of the areas in which these indigenous peoples have lived for generations.

It will be worth our while, therefore, to look at the experience of Amerindians in some South American countries in a little more detail. There are two main reasons for this. Firstly, it is an issue which transcends national boundaries. Many South American countries share a similar experience of contact with previously unknown groups, resulting from determined expansion into the largely unmapped Amazon region. Secondly, the underlying causes of the spreading conflict are typical: the exploitation of wealth, the consolidation of power and, as a result, the spread of influence.

In January 1986, Survival International listed the campaigns in which it was involved in defence of Amerindians' rights. As Box 5 shows, these covered every country on the continent, apart from Argentina, Bolivia, Surinam and Uruguay.

The brief descriptions in Box 5 also outline a common thread linking the campaigns by the various Amerindian peoples — namely their right to the land which has been traditionally theirs. The origins of the immediate threat to these land rights may well vary. For example, the threat has originated from mineral prospectors, mining and oil companies, cattle ranchers and peasant farmers. On a number of occasions, the Amerindians' difficulties have been caused or compounded by the actions of governments, including at least one instance where the government has failed to ensure that they have legally recognised title to the land on which they live. This both undermines their security and increases the likelihood of violent clashes between different groups competing for control of the same resource — land.

Any attempt to explain these governmental failures must be tentative. However, two broad themes may be said to permeate the thinking behind present-day policy or, more frequently, the lack of policy. Firstly, there appears to have been an almost total official ignorance of the existence of many of the Amerindian people. For example, when the Brazilian government decided during the 1960s to embark on the expansion into the Amazon basin, it publicised and promoted the opening up of the area, describing it as a programme designed to guarantee land for people "in a land without people".

Box 5: The threat to Amerindian peoples

Affected Amerindian groups

Brazil
Attempt by 3,000 miners to invade the Yanomami Indians' land resisted while seven-year demarcation campaign continues.
Five thousand Indians under threat from Grande Carajas, especially the Tucurui Dam and chemical defoliants.
Apinaye Indians in conflict with peasant squatters owing to government failure to demarcate lands in Carajas Project.
Pataxo' Ha-Ha-Hai lands encroached on by local ranchers.
Txukarrame hold government officials hostage in attempt to secure their land rights.
Elf oil company forced to compensate for illegal intrusion on to Satere-Maue land.
Polonoreste project threatens 8,000 Indians in 32 groups with land losses; World Bank withholds loan.
Kaingang Indians demand the return of their traditional lands.
Petroleum prospectors invade Javari Valley; government Indian agency revokes oil contract.

Chile
One million Mapuche Indians organise to resist government oppression.

Colombia
Paez and Guambiano Indians massacred as Indian councils seek to protect their lands from encroachment by non-Indian landlords.

Subsequently, it became perfectly clear that the land was already occupied but this discovery did not alter the overall policy adopted. More recently, similar apparent ignorance has been displayed by the government of Peru. In the early 1980s the last remaining unspoilt area of the Amuesha Indians' homeland, the Palcazu Valley, was included within the scope of the Pichis-Palcuza development project, largely funded by USAID. In the initial planning phase, the government insisted that the valley was unpopulated — despite the fact that between 10,000 and 15,000 people lived there, 3,000 of whom were Amuesha Indians. Even when the true state of affairs had been brought to its attention, no concern was displayed concerning the community's needs. Despite the provision of a US$18 million loan for Indian community development, final plans for land use, management and health care lumped the Amuesha together with all the other inhabitants of the valley, ignoring, says Survival International, the special needs of the

Sikuani Indian lands threatened by cattle ranching and colonists.

Ecuador
Oil companies and settlers invade lands of isolated Waoroni Indians.

French Guiana
Government to resettle Indians in special villages.

Guyana
Development projects and boundary disputes delay settlement of Indian land claims.

Paraguay
US fundamentalist New Tribes missionaries pose threat to previously nomadic Ayoreo Indians.

Panama
Eighty thousand Guaymi Indians struggle for ownership of traditional land and resist Rio Tinto Zinc copper mine.

Peru
Pichis-Palcazu road-building and colonisation project threatens Amuesha Indians; project modified following protests.

Venezuela
Piaroa Indians in conflict with ranchers; Indian land claims upheld by government.

Indian minority and the recommendations made to USAID and the Peruvian Government in the specially commissioned 800-page report on the area.

This suggests that the view that Amerindian peoples are backward, anti-development and needing to be acculturalised by the society as a whole, was the determining factor in the development of policy towards them. The view itself may stem from one of two approaches. On the one hand, it is possible that the government's attitude was paternalistic. There is some evidence to suggest that this may be the case, since many Latin American countries have demarcated land as the preserve of indigenous peoples. The creation of reservations, pioneered in Brazil by the Villas Boas brothers, this creation of reservations mirrored similar policies in the United States and in the African colonies of the European powers. It was based on the desire to protect the Amerindians, and other indigenous peoples, from the loss of their land through sale or invasion by other members of the society. Thus, typically, ownership of the land, where it was demarcated, was retained by the authorities. At best, this was misguided paternalism as it demonstrates a perception of indigenous people as unable to manage their own affairs. At worst, this policy could degenerate into gross exploitation (see Case Study 4 at the end of this section) and the limitation of land access for political and economic reasons (see *Land and Poverty*, CAFOD, 1987).

Photo: Victor Englebert/Survival International

The Yanomami Indians of Brazil are struggling to survive and maintain their habitat and lifestyle in the face of an influx of mineral prospectors and gold-panners, who destroy the forest and pollute rivers.

It is possible, on the other hand, that Latin American governments and people regard the Amerindian peoples, who shun contact with present-day society, as sub-human, barely better than animals. In Ecuador, for example, uncontacted groups of the Waoroni are referred to as *auca* (naked savages) by settled Indians and other members of the society. But the Waoroni have good reason to fear contact with modern society. It has been calculated that, since 1956, one in six Waoroni have died, half of them having been shot by outsiders who have also stolen children for use as servants. The experience of the Totobiegosode Indians of Paraguay has been even more dehumanising. With the help of a helicopter belonging to missionaries of the evangelical Protestant New Tribes Mission, a Totobiegosode group was tracked down by 34 Christian (also referred to as "tame") Indians in December 1986. Fearful of being attacked, as on similar occasions in the past, the Totobiegosode themselves attacked the approaching Indians, killing five and wounding a number of others. Twenty-four Totobeigosode were captured and brought forcibly back to the mission station. Within days, four of them had to be hospitalised, suffering from influenza to which they had no resistance because of their previous isolation.

If such attitudes towards Amerindian and other indigenous peoples prevail, they would explain the apparent disregard with which many governments pursue their country's development, and the seeming lack of concern displayed at events such as those described above. In this connection it is worth noting that the Paraguayan government, whose motives were clearly economic, enlisted the help of the New Tribes Mission's to "settle and civilise" the Indians who had frustrated the search for oil and gas deposits on their land. Efforts to exploit the mineral wealth of traditional Amerindian lands have been at the root of conflicts with prospectors in other countries too.

In Ecuador the Waoroni Indians have clashed repeatedly in the past with oil prospectors, and the clashes increased in number following the government's opening of several new oil exploration concessions to the major international companies. The effects of the companies' activities since the late 1960s explain much of the Waoroni violence towards outsiders: the game on which the Indians depend for their food has been driven out of the areas around the drilling; colonists, making use of the company roads, have invaded the forest and settled on the best land; and oil spills from pipelines have polluted the rivers and destroyed the fish.

Tragically, even those attempting to contact the Waoroni with the best of intentions have become victims of this violence. In July 1987, Mgr Alejandro Labaca, Bishop of Coca in the Amazonia diocese and Iñes Arango were murdered by a group of Waoroni with whom they were trying to make contact. That Mgr Labaca and Sr Iñes were fully aware of the dangers of their attempt is shown by the letter which the bishop left behind, pleading that there should be no reprisals against Indians if he were killed during his efforts to protect them from outsiders.

Nor were the oil companies unaware of the Indians' attitude to their activities. Before the murder of Mgr Labaca and Sr Iñes, the Ecuadorian state oil company, CEPE, drew up a "project to contact the Waoroni", which states explicitly: "As the Indians do not want to let the exploration teams in [to their lands], the oil companies must draw up a project to tranquilise the Waoroni's spirit and make them participate in the exploration." Such an approach shows little reassurance that the oil companies will adopt the necessary safeguards to prevent ongoing pollution and destruction of the environment on which Indian groups depend for their livelihood. This is of particular concern, given the likelihood that the Ecuadorian government will open the southern part of Ecuadorian Amazonia, the homelands of the Shuar and Achuar, to oil exploration in the near future.

In eastern Bolivia's Amazon forests, the estimated 140 remaining nomadic Yuqui (the other 110 have been settled at the New Tribes Mission, Chimore) face, according to Survival International, virtual extinction at the hands of oil prospectors, loggers and colonists. This last remnant is said to be particularly threatened by loggers, who are determined to clear the Yuqui from the area so that the tropical hardwoods can be exploited. Survival International reports that the Yuqui are being hunted down and shot by loggers who claim to be acting in self-defence. A similar report was received from the Brazilian state of Amazonas, where a party of unarmed Indians were allegedly ambushed by gunmen, hired by a local timber merchant, on 28 March 1988. At least ten Ticuna Indian men and two children were murdered in the attack.

All of these activities are illegal in the countries in which they occur. However, inadequate central government control, the need to generate wealth (not least to service the national debt), the incompetence and often corruption of local officials, and individual greed have combined to undermine the interests of minorities such as the Amerindians. And societal attitudes, which appear to regard uncontacted Amerindians as little more than animals, are unlikely to alter this. Reports of similar attacks on indigenous peoples were commonplace in frontier regions of the United States, Canada and Australia during the nineteenth century.

Criticism directed at aid donors should be careful not to overlook policies designed to defend the rights of indigenous peoples. In the case of the Pichis-Palcazu development project (see p.99), the major aid donor, USAID, both commissioned a study of the proposed project's impact on the Amuesha Indian community and made an additional loan available specifically for Indian Community Development Programmes. Similarly, the World Bank now routinely insists that there should be a study of any Bank-supported project's impact on indigenous people, and adequate development assistance to enable affected groups to overcome the negative effects of the programme and improve the quality of their lives. However, a gap remains between the design of policies and their implementation although the British government and groups such as Survival International, and NGOs, like CAFOD and Oxfam, have done much to ensure that this now happens more often.

Possibly the most successful example to date is the Indian Narmada Valley Development Scheme, where locally organised groups of tribal people have been able to secure some guarantees of future compensation for their proposed loss of land (see Chapter 3, pp.47-48). However, much more needs to be done. It is all too easy for governments with other priorities to ignore the interests of minorities and the demands of aid donor organisations' headquarters.

All the same, a word of caution is needed. Well-intentioned efforts to protect indigenous peoples from the worst effects of a modernising economy can result in their further disempowerment, if not the destruction of their culture. In any case, some members of these indigenous societies will wish to avail themselves of the benefits available in the wider society. One of the reasons for the San peoples' decision to leave the Gemsbok Reserve (see Case Study 4) was the South African authorities' refusal to allow them to engage in cattle and sheep ranching. And it is likely that those Amerindians who have chosen to settle around mission stations were partly motivated by the chance to improve the quality of their lives through access to health and education facilities.

Denying people the right to make and implement decisions which will lead to an improvement in the quality of their lives is not only dehumanising but also likely to result in increased tensions within the group, which in turn may easily result in its disintegration. Thus, it seems necessary to create conditions which prevent exploitation while allowing the people to make their own choices — and to do so within a framework which results in the improvement of the quality of life of the whole population.

This is difficult to achieve, but the chances of so doing have improved in recent years. The development of a body representing many of Brazil's Indian groups, and the election of an Amerindian to the Brazilian congress, are signs that the means to bring about "democratic discussion amongst all sectors of Brazilian society" exist, even if only in embryonic form. And the growing willingness of indigenous peoples to organise amongst themselves on a national, and increasingly an international, scale suggests that the same is true in many other countries.

The relative paucity of such discussion to date indicates a lack of political will on the part of many third world governments which may have its root in societal attitudes towards indigenous people. A change in attitude is not something which can be legislated but government action can assist the process. A possible first step would be for the relevant governments were to vest control over their land in the people themselves.

Exploiting the world's resources

Broadly speaking, the world's resources can be divided into the finite and the renewable. Humanity as a whole utilises both but the potential for using particular resources is to a considerable extent determined by the level of technological development which a society has achieved. The recent past has seen an explosion of scientific understanding and this has not only added to the exploitation of the world's resources but also permitted their redefinition. For example, resources, such as coal or oil, which must have seemed infinite to our ancestors of 100 or so years ago, are now recognisably finite. On the other hand, scientific advances now permit adaptations of the genetic components of life to build in immunity or greater resistance to known diseases and pests, greater levels of production, adaptability to particular climatic conditions, and so on.

CAFOD's view of the important problems arising from these developments has already been indicated briefly in the discussion of the Green Revolution in the Punjab (pp.46-48), but it is worth expanding on it here. Firstly, the Green Revolution package was precisely that. The seeds alone would not result in higher yields. And the package was beyond the means of many small farmers, tenant farmers and sharecroppers who did not have the necessary cash available to buy all its parts. The benefits thus went to larger farmers, and the gap between rich and poor widened. That gap became wider still as landlords found it more profitable to farm their land themselves rather than rent it out, and sharecroppers and tenant farmers found that they no longer had access to land. There was also a decline in the availability of regular agricultural jobs as farmers switched to more mechanised forms of production. Thus, although agricultural wages rose in many cases, rural incomes as a whole declined, resulting in still greater rural poverty and further encouraging the drift towards the towns.

Secondly, the seeds' need for regular supplies of water led to the entrenchment of unequal power relationships in many countries. In order to guarantee regular supplies of water, irrigation systems had to be established. The many wells which were sunk and dams which were built were frequently on land owned by large landowners, who regarded them as their own. They allowed others access to the necessary water, but in many cases only at a price. This further increased their own wealth and power in the local community. What is more, as reports from CAFOD's partner organisation in India, Caritas India, have shown (see p.48), in the longer term the extent of irrigation has seriously depleted underground water reserves, while waterlogging and increased salinity have reduced the fertility of the soil.

Third, the need to make use of biocides (pesticides, herbicides and fungicides) resulted in many cases of pollution and the need to apply larger and larger quantities of pesticides to maintain production levels. Thus, Thai farmers who used the weed killer Paraquat in accordance with the instructions they received, found that it leached into the country's rivers, killing the fish which had formed a cheap source of protein for the rural people. And in the Sudan more and more pesticides have to be applied to the country's cotton crop as pests develop greater levels of resistance. The leaching of fertilisers into rivers and streams has resulted in rapid aquatic plant growth, which ultimately de-oxygenates the rivers and streams, reducing their capacity to sustain life.

Lastly, the increased use of high-yielding seeds poses potential dangers because of their uniformity. The decline in the number of food sources from over 1,500 species of plants during prehistoric times to only 20 species used in field production today is risky, according to botanists such as Pat Mooney, Carey Fowler and Henk Hobbelink. Single-species cultivation has already resulted in massive crop losses. The Irish potato famine of the 1840s originated from the destruction of the crop by a new disease which attacked a single variety of potato. More recent examples of single-species vulnerability saw 65% of the North American durum wheat crop destroyed by disease in 1953; the destruction of the entire spring wheat crop of the Sacramento Valley in 1974; the infestation of 20% of the Zambian maize crop with a new type of mould in the same year; and the virtual destruction of the entire Indian millet crop.

Crop losses on this scale are bearable, if only just. But the possibility of still greater uniformity coupled with the rapid evolution of new diseases and pests with higher resistance to known pesticides, could lead to far greater losses, pricing many millions more out of survival.

This brings us to a further cause for concern. According to an international agricultural expert, Professor M. Dambroth, the genetic erosion now taking place is largely due to developments like the Green Revolution. And this raises questions concerning who owns these resources, since the supply of a product is determined, under economic theory, by the desire and ability to pay (the demand) for it.

Location of genetic resources
Virtually everything that we eat can be traced to 11 centres of wide genetic diversity. Named after the Russian botanist who dominated the study of plants in the early years of this century, the Vavilov centres are all located in the Third World, with the partial exception of that which focuses on the Mediterranean Sea. (The spread of glaciers, during the Ice Age, is believed to be the reason why no Vavilov centres exist in the North.) The existence in these centres of numerous varieties of the same plant are explained by localised climatic differences. Human action, including the selection of the highest yielding strains in particular areas and cross-breeding to increase yields over the centuries, further developed the plants. And the migration of people spread food, and other plants, across the globe.

The emergence of farming as a profitable operation brought in its

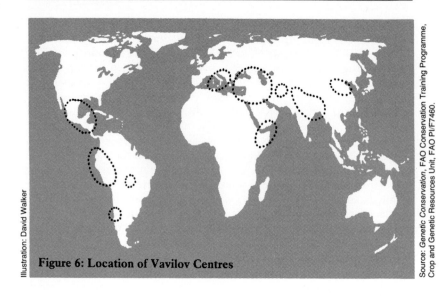

Illustration: David Walker

Source: *Genetic Conservation*, FAO Conservation Training Programme, Crop and Genetic Resources Unit, FAO PI/F7460.

Figure 6: Location of Vavilov Centres

train the development of agricultural supply industries. Thus, most farmers found it worth their while to buy seed from a supplier rather than develop it themselves as their predecessors had done. The advent of the Green Revolution package further enhanced the process of distancing the individual farmer from all stages in the production of his crop. Indeed, the commercialisation of agriculture, in which the Green Revolution and later biotechnological developments have played an important part, significantly increased the pace at which this distancing occurs.

The early years of the Green Revolution witnessed the emergence of fewer, and much larger, seed companies as small companies were taken over by more profitable concerns. These were then taken over in their turn by still larger organisations, many of which had previously showed little, if any, direct interest in agriculture. At this stage, many of the world's major oil transnational corporations bought up seed companies, rationalising this development as a logical outgrowth of their production of fertilisers. More recently, the oil companies have begun divesting their interests but this has not meant an upsurge in the number of seed companies, merely a change of ownership.

Corporate interest in the seeds business is based on two factors. One is obvious — profit. But the seed companies' profits are protected and enhanced by the legal possibility of patenting at least some forms of life. Originating in the US Plant Patenting Act of the 1930s, which allowed the patenting of non-sexually reproduced varieties of plants, the ability to patent life was further enhanced by the creation in the early 1960s of the Union for the Protection of New Varieties of Plants (UPOV). This established specialised plant-breeders' rights, applicable to "varieties" only, and granted exclusive control over the marketing and sale of the patented variety.

There were, nonetheless, strict limits to plant breeders' rights. Although researchers had to pay royalties to the owner of the patent, they were still able to make use of the patented variety to develop others. Similarly, farmers were allowed to re-use part of their harvest as seed, where this was possible. Lastly, any variety patented under the UPOV convention could not also be patented under national legislation, thereby preventing so-called "double protection". The determination of plant breeders' rights reflected a serious compromise of different interests. However, little direct attention was paid to the needs of third world countries in which the genetic resources originated and from which they are continually collected. These countries' interests were meant to be safeguarded by the FAO, which established a series of internationally-controlled stores of genetic resources and at whose meetings regular discussion of the free exchange of genetic resources occurs.

Recent developments have considerably widened the definition of what is patentable. US legislation in 1985 and again in 1987 permitted the patenting both of plants (rather than varieties of plants) and of animals. Moreover, not only is the plant itself patentable, but so are its characteristics. Thus a US company, Sungene, has patented a sunflower with the characteristic of a "high oil-content" and has written to all its competitors warning them that it will regard any sunflower with a high oil-content as an infringement of this patent. Similarly, another US company has patented a variety of maize which it developed to overproduce the amino acid, tryptophane; the legislation means that any other maize plant which does this automatically impinges on the patent.

The US is not the only activist in this area, although it does lead the field: a recent draft EC directive, a copy of which CAFOD has obtained, threatens to enable European firms to patent life. According to Henk Hobbelink, the co-ordinator of the International Coalition for Development Action's Seeds Programme, a CAFOD-supported project, there are a number of problems associated with this. He argues that the directive goes considerably further than existing US legislation.

Firstly, there is no upper limit on what life can be patented; thus, if the directive is adopted as it currently stands, human beings could be patented. This is undoubtedly an oversight and will be speedily corrected, but other provisions of the draft are equally worrying. Secondly envisages permitting the patenting of processes and techniques which lie at the basis of plant and animal breeding as industrial activities. Thirdly, it calls for the patentability of products, which would allow the patenting of whole families or types of plants and animals. Fourthly, farmers would no longer be permitted to re-use part of their harvest as seed. This would make illegal the activities of the co-operatives which collect, clean and prepare farmers' seed.

Fifthly, with the extension of patent rights envisaged in the draft, plant and animal breeding would become enmeshed in a net of existing patents. This would substantially increase the cost of new seeds because of the need to make royalty payments at practically every stage of the process. Furthermore, as in the US, characteristics of plants and animals would be patentable. Lastly, the directive would make a nonsense of the FAO discussions about the free exchange of genetic resources and effectively put an end to the efforts of third world countries to regain control over their botanical wealth.

The final version of the EC directive, adopted in October 1988 and sent to member governments for inclusion within national legislation, is, according to Hobbelink, even more inclined towards the needs of industry. For example, whereas the draft had envisaged some protection of the rights, albeit at a price, of plant breeders, the final version undermines the breeder's right to include a patented gene in any new plant variety, and this is more closely aligned to US legislation. Furthermore, the EC is reported to be encouraging member governments to introduce the necessary national legislation as soon as possible. This is not particularly surprising, since intellectual property rights are an important focus for the negotiations now under way in the Uruguay Round of the General Agreement on Tariffs and Trade (GATT).

Developments such as these clearly demonstrate that the patent debate is currently preoccupied with the interests of industry. It may be that the recent developments in biotechnology have made existing legislation outdated, but to give priority to the biotechnology industry's need to become profitable at the earliest opportunity is cynicism of the highest order. In the past, patent legislation and practice reflected a compromise, however imperfect, between the interests of industry and those of society at large. This is clearly lacking in the current proposals.

Technology and development

The expression of these concerns should not be misinterpreted. Advances in biotechnology are potentially as beneficial in the development process as those in any other sphere of human activity. What is in question here is the appropriateness of the particular technology as well as its ownership. Although discussion so far has focused on technological advances in agriculture, one may illustrate questions relating to technological appropriateness in other fields as well. The health sector is one area of substantial recent advances. One such concerned the discovery of a vaccine against hepatitis B, a highly contagious disease, transmitted *inter alia* through blood and blood products, and unsterilised syringes. The company which developed the vaccine patented its discovery, and was able to set a price on it which allowed the fast recovery of its research costs and ensured that it was an important profit earner. Thus, despite the fact that over half of those infected with hepatitis B live in the Pacific region, the company developed the vaccine with the North American market in mind, and priced it accordingly. This situation has been described by officials of the World Health Organisation (WHO) as a scandal, since it places profits before people. As John Elkington of the Washington-based World Resources Institute observes, such a vaccine "may eventually be used in the Third World, once the initial investment has been recouped", but he notes that "this 'trickle down' approach to the problem of applying biotechnology to third world problems is seen as inadequate".[14] Dr Jonathan Mann, senior WHO official and co-ordinator of its programme on AIDS, is far less careful in his choice of words. Dr Mann is adamant that in order to prevent a recurrence of the hepatitis B vaccine scandal the technological advances required to attack the AIDS virus successfully must be the property of the international community as a whole.

WHO's insistence on public ownership of vaccines, so that people, rather than company profits, are the major beneficiaries, is based on its experience of dealing with the giant pharmaceutical companies. For example, one US corporation ended WHO research into an anti-malaria vaccine, partly because of difficulties associated with its development, but also because of a dispute between the company and the WHO over ownership of the research results.

As already indicated, such concerns of appropriateness and ownership apply to the agricultural sector too. As Dr Robert Goodman, vice-president of Calgene Inc, a US company active in developing plants with resistance to specific herbicides, expressed it: "The strongest programmes in biotechnology are in the hands of commercial sector laboratories. How will their proprietary technical abilities be brought to commercially unrewarding but highly-vital improvements of agriculture in the developing nations?" This question is particularly important in the light of the direction of research and development of companies such as Calgene.

Farmers utilising seeds treated by the Calgene process are able to make use of glyphosphate, one of the world's largest selling, and reputedly environmentally-safer, herbicides, without risking contamination of their product. Such research and development is clearly beneficial, but is it particularly relevant to the needs of third world farmers? It may be more appropriate that research and development should focus on genetic adaptations which match crops to local conditions — for example maximising production under arid conditions, crops resistant to common local pests and diseases, and which do not require large amounts of high-cost, additional inputs.

Some companies are engaged in such research. Calgene, for example, is also engaged in research designed to develop major crop plants resistant to viral diseases which cannot be treated with chemicals; and it also plans to move on to research on fungal and bacterial diseases. But the size of the herbicide industry (approximately US$4.5 billion a year), the relative poverty of the biotechnology industry, and the fact that the latter is largely owned by profit-orientated private corporations suggest that there is considerable substance in the criticism advanced by many third world countries that the industry is mainly interested in the further development of herbicide-resistant plants and crops such as soya or tobacco, whose exploitation can be maximised commercially. In other words, the industry tends to follow the maxim of Calgene president, Dr Jerry Caulder: "If you want to collect manure, you have got to follow the elephant, not the sparrows". Thus, to date the biotechnology industry has favoured high-value markets, paying little attention to the conservation of genetic diversity, sustainable development or the needs of third world farmers.

One of the reasons for this has already been explained — the industry's need to be commercially viable. But the apparent lack of attention to sustainable development practices is, according to John Elkington, as much due to biotechnologists' lack of awareness of the links between their companies' future prosperity and the fate of the world's genetic resources, as to the failure of those engaged in the promotion of sustainable development to have a clear picture of the industry. This view is also held by Dr John McIntyre, of yet another US company, Ecogen, who has observed that many biotechnology companies are small enough to profit from their involvement in projects valued at as little as US$1 million.

Nonetheless, the challenge remains clear: how can one ensure that the industry participates fully in what are often commercially unattractive programmes? What is needed is a means of making sure that the benefits of technology can be enjoyed by all the world's peoples, rather than only by those who are wealthy enough to pay for them. One such means could be greater public subsidy of the costs of research programmes — though in such a case ownership of the results of any research would have to be placed in public hands — and, to neutralise international rivalries, international organisations such as the WHO or the FAO would have to be the legal owners of the world's "intellectual property".

This may appear a utopian ideal at present, although there are international agreements (such as that which regulates the use of the Antarctic, the Law of the Sea and the EC directive on the disposal of waste) which recognise the principle of common ownership or mutual responsibility. However, until such time as the international community accepts that the world's genetic resources are the common property of all people, the possibilities that technology can assist the sustainable development process are limited.

As we noted above, many individual companies in the biotechnology industry are able to profit from relatively low-cost projects. It appears necessary, therefore, that these companies and other agents active in the development process should investigate possible areas of mutually beneficial collaboration. Moreover, it is crucial that the results of such collaboration should be affordable by third world people. One of the

Photo: Mark Edwards/Still Pictures

Sowing seeds, Ethiopia. For genetic research to benefit third world farmers, it must concentrate on adapting crops to local conditions.

ways in which this could be assured would be for those involved in such research to demonstrate their acceptance of the important contribution made by the Third World to the research. Without the germplasm available in the Vavilov Centres, for instance, the research would be very much more difficult, if not impossible in many cases.

Such an acceptance would provide a firm foundation for the development of a spirit of partnership which, according to the Brundtland Commission, is essential for a sustainable development policy for the world as a whole. Without a recognition of the need for such a partnership, there are few grounds for believing that human achievements will be equally beneficial to all.

What emerges from the above is that, for good or ill, the contribution of human beings is crucial. By their actions they can seriously damage the environment (take, for example the expanded aid programmes to Sahelian countries after the 1973/74 famine, or the intensification of copper production on Marinduque island), or they can protect and improve it — which is what has happened in the case of Cape Verde and the community-based reforestation programmes of the Green Belt Movement. Since the greatest successes have occurred where all parties involved have a shared interest in the development process, it is important to deal early with any conflict of interests. Once they have resolved their differences, those involved will be more likely to take a long-term view of such matters as the rate of return on an investment, the siting of a development project, or the criteria by which success or failure should be judged.

Attempts to protect the environment are least successful when there is no recognised common interest — this is particularly evident where the desire for economic modernisation and national integration conflict with the needs of indigenous peoples. What is more, failure to discover what is in the general interest can lead to technological advances that are of doubtful value, not only to the Third World but also to the First. And finally, it is responsible for many of the environmentally destructive practices of poor people, whose need forces them to do things that ultimately militate against the interests of others, as well as their own.

The obstacles to recognition of a common interest are largely political. Powerful groups, like the Marcopper Mining Corporation and the Marinduque Mining and Industrial Corporation, are anxious to maintain the *status quo*, and carry more weight with the Philippines Government than does a poor fishing community. Likewise in Brazil the fate of the Amerindian peoples — not to mention the rain forest in which they live — invariably takes second place when the interests of large landowners, foreign investors and a government anxious for foreign exchange are at stake.

It may be that an important, if barely formulated, reason for actions such as those discussed above stems from the development model's rejection of the expertise of the majority of third world people. This has meant that, at best, these people have not benefited to the extent which they might have done; and, at worst, that they have been shunted aside over the past four decades. There are signs that this may be changing, albeit slowly and due very largely to the actions of the people themselves. And the changes which have occurred have clarified the need for popular support for and participation in the development process. It seems safe to say that the prospects for sustainable development — guaranteeing an ongoing improvement in the quality of life — will be enhanced where such a spirit of partnership prevails. In the concluding chapter, therefore, the meaning of development will be explored in greater detail.

Notes

14. John Elkington, *Double Dividends: US Biotechnology and Third World Development*, World Resources Institute (Washington, 1986).

CASE STUDY FOUR

CONSERVING TO EXTINCTION: THE BUSHMEN OF SOUTH AFRICA AND NAMIBIA

The South African government forcibly tried to conserve the San Peoples — not least because of their perceived "tourist value".

Conservation is frequently thought to be, *ipso facto*, "a good thing". Through the adoption of conservation policies, we are able to demonstrate a "nobler" side of human nature, a caring for species and peoples less able to survive than we are ourselves. However, as the anthropologist Robert J Gordon points out, concepts such as "heritage" and "traditional" are cultural interpretations which dominant groups within a society impose on weaker groups.[15]

In support of his argument, Gordon cites the experience of the San people of South Africa and Namibia. These people, believed by many to have been the earliest inhabitants of the region, were hunter-gatherers. This way of life requires access to considerable areas of land and frequently brought the San into conflict with later arrivals, who followed a more settled pattern either of pastoralism or of settled agriculture. The history of the San peoples after the arrival of both African and European settlers is one of constant retreat into the region's less environmentally hospitable areas and of considerable hostility from people following a more settled lifestyle. Oral history recounts a massacre of a large group of San by Bantu-speaking Africans in what is today Angola during the eighteenth century; and in south-eastern parts of present-day South Africa, organised hunts of San people were carried out by Boer settlers during the latter stages of the same century. Despite this hostility, which frequently originated in the San practice of hunting and killing the cattle and sheep of the more settled peoples, there was also frequent contact with more settled groups and inter-marriage with Bantu-speaking Africans.

By the time of the 1936 Empire Exhibition in South Africa, at which a group of San were displayed as the "seventh wonder of southern Africa" and "living fossils", the San peoples remaining in South Africa lived in the Kalahari desert, on the borders of modern Botswana. Considerable efforts were made at this time to establish a reserve in which they could live "traditionally".

In practice this meant that the 12,000 morgen (approximately 10,125 hectares) which was set aside could only be inhabited by "genuine Bushmen", as the San were commonly called. The liberal South African minister of native affairs in the 1940s, Denys Reitz, summed up the official attitude when he told the South African parliament in 1941:

It would be a biological crime if we allowed such a peculiar race to die out, because it is a race which looks more like a baboon than a baboon itself does...we have so far got about 29 who are just about genuine. It is difficult to say what a genuine Bushman looks like. These 29 Bushmen are now in the Gemsbok (Nature) Reserve, and it is our intention to leave them there and to allow them to hunt with bows and arrows but without dogs. We look upon them as part of the fauna of the country. The Bushmen are now close to Le Riche's [the game warden's] house in the Gemsbok Reserve. He is trying to tame them at the moment.

These San clearly found the restrictions placed on them unsatisfactory. They made increasing demands on the authorities for, *inter alia*, greater freedom to hunt and the right to hunt with dogs, freedom of movement, and, worst of all from the perspective of the conservationists, better housing. Nor was this all, for the conservationists were soon complaining that the San were intermarrying with other groups and were thus no longer "genuine Bushmen". And H Kloppers, in his book about Joep le Riche's work as warden of the Gemsbok Reserve, was uncompromising: "Their desirability as a tourist attraction is under serious doubt, as is the desirability of letting them stay for an indefinite period in the park. They have disqualified themselves."

The San, however, took matters into their own hands. All had left the park by 1982 for neighbouring Botswana, where they were able to pursue their own development, raising herds of sheep and cattle, rather than forming a tourist attraction in a game reserve.

Attitudes like this are characteristic not only of the racism prevalent in South Africa: justifications for the creation of similar reserves for Brazilian Amerindians were along the same lines, and formed a major part of anthropological theory at the time. However, this does not explain what happened in Namibia in 1984.

In July of that year, the illegal South African administration declared the 562,000 hectares of the Kalahari desert on the western border of Botswana, known as Bushmanland, a national park. The San, who lived in the area, were to be allowed to continue to do so. But although they had made known their wish to keep livestock and generally improve their living conditions through better housing, this was not allowed, largely on the grounds that stock-raising was not environmentally sustainable. This claim was made despite the absence of any reference to an ecological study of the region in official reports between 1975 and 1981.

The only occupation which the San were to be allowed to undertake was hunting and gathering, thereby preserving their "heritage" and "traditional way of life", even though such preservation is more akin to fossilisation and is carried out in the interests of promoting tourism. The World Bank explicitly warns against policies which promote "enforced primitivism", either as a means of promoting tourism or as a way of "preserving a tribe's cultural identity" for the reasons cited above.

Notes

15. "Conserving Bushmen to Extinction in Southern Africa", in *An End to Laughter: Tribal Peoples and Economic Development, Survival Internation Review*, No.44, 1985.

CHAPTER 6

CONCLUSION: TOWARDS A DEFINITION OF DEVELOPMENT

The question we have been trying to answer here is: how far have the theory and practice of development during the past four decades led to true development? In many ways the answer we have come up with is positive. There can be no doubt that the world's wealth has increased overall; and no doubt either, that the majority of people have seen an improvement, albeit small, in the quality of their lives. What is more, statistics like those contained in the World Bank's annual *World Development Report* indicate that average life expectancy has increased, as have the average availability of medical services and the average level of literacy. While it is difficult to say exactly how development aid, and particularly official development aid from international institutions and donor governments, has been responsible for this, it clearly has made a contribution in the short term at least.

Nonetheless, we have also seen that there have been costs associated with it. In Indonesia, for example, aid programmes such as the transmigration programme have resulted in considerable environmental destruction and a worsening quality of life for the people already living in the areas of settlement as well as for the majority of migrants. Similar effects have been noted in Brazil and India, while at least one proposed development project in Africa, the southern Sudan's Jonglei Canal, has been an important cause not only of environmental degradation but, more immediately, of the negation of a region's development potential through civil war. We have also seen how the development model, emphasising an export-oriented modern economy, has been associated with the rapid expansion of third world indebtedness; and that the same institutions which lent the money now insist that it be repaid, often with what looks like scant regard for the human or environmental cost.

We have questioned whether such effects can truly be regarded as development, or whether the policies which produce them should not rather be seen as attempts to maximise short-term profits without regard for the future. If the latter is the case, then it cannot truly be considered as development — at least not the development of people. For development implies that both present and future generations benefit from economic advance and that no single generation should knowingly act in such a way as to create avoidable problems for its heirs.

It must be admitted that these questions are not particularly original. To its credit, the environmental movement throughout the world, and particularly in the United States, has been asking similar questions for

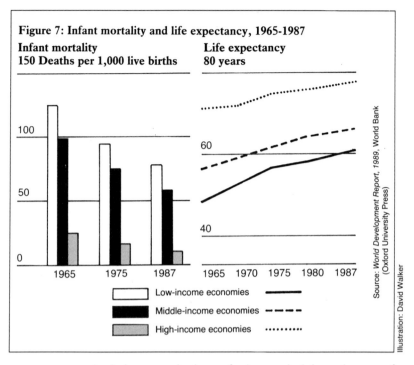

Figure 7: Infant mortality and life expectancy, 1965-1987

Infant mortality
150 Deaths per 1,000 live births

Life expectancy
80 years

Low-income economies
Middle-income economies
High-income economies

Source: *World Development Report, 1989*, World Bank (Oxford University Press)

Illustration: David Walker

many years. And its questioning of the underlying theory of conventional development has encouraged institutions such as the World Bank and official donor organisations to reconsider their project criteria. This process received a further boost with the establishment of the Brundtland Commission and the publication of its findings in *Our Common Future*, while, internally, the Bank has produced a better-staffed environment department and an agreed work programme.

Not a moment too soon, you might say. But it might be fairer to regard it as a sign that, for all its monolithic appearance, the Bank, like so many other institutions, is made up of people who both care for and, possibly more importantly, listen to the concerns of others. Having said that, a note of caution is necessary in this regard: with the best will in the world, the Bank's new orientation will inevitably take some time to make a visible impact. It may well have set itself an agenda for the next 30 years, simply correcting the mistakes of the past; and, given human fallibility, it is likely that mistakes will be made in the future too.

That problems will result from the interaction of humanity and the environment is inevitable. As we saw in the discussion on the causes of desertification in Africa's Sahel region, even the best planned development projects have run into problems which were not envisaged at the time of implementation. And it is important to remember that people's actions have always affected their environment. For example,

farmers have selected seeds for replanting which were best suited to their environment, thereby reducing the genetic resource base of the area in which they lived. Similarly, wild animals were domesticated and put to use as draught animals or as stores of food and wealth. Farmers have also made use of natural products — human and animal dung or compost — to increase and maintain the soil's fertility and rivers have been dammed to ensure a supply of water for irrigation purposes. There is nothing intrinsically wrong in humanity having an effect on the environment in which it lives. In many instances this effect may well be positive.

Few would argue that programmes such as that of the Kenyan Green Belt Movement or the government of Cape Verde are destructive of the environment. But it is undeniable that their successful implementation will have an effect on the environment. The ultimate aim of the Cape Verde programme is to transform the archipelago into lush, green oases — an effective change in the micro-climate — thereby ensuring improvements in the inhabitants' quality of life. One can only speculate upon the wider implications of this; it may be that if Cape Verde receives more rain, mainland Sahelian countries will receive less. Such a result would be regrettable, but is it a reason for the Cape Verdians to abandon their efforts to improve the environment and, hence, their descendants' chances of a better life than they now enjoy?

To argue that they should abandon the scheme is clearly a counsel of despair and, as such, is instinctively rejected by the vast majority of people, for whom hope is a major motivating force in their efforts to improve the quality of their lives. Only hope can explain why thousands of Africans left their homes and walked hundreds of miles in search of food during the recent famine; hope was at the root of their efforts to recreate their lives; and hope for a better future for African people undoubtedly inspired the generous assistance from others around the world. But this does not mean that hope should be blind. Indeed, the fact that people's actions will affect their environment suggests that their hope should be as well-informed as possible.

This need is now more urgent because of the greater scale of such human impact. Whereas, in earlier times, the environmental impact of technological capabilities was limited or localised, the expansion of technological advance over the past 150 years has meant that humanity's impact on the environment has multiplied in extent. For example, it is now feasible to mine the Antarctic, a technological advance not dreamed of at the beginning of the century and regarded as just a dream as recently as the 1960s. At the same time, humanity's ability to harm the environment through both its expanded technological capability and its failure to reorientate its thinking to

◄ *A reforestation programme in Ethiopia. True development must involve real partnership with communities in developing countries, allowing them to identify their needs, plan and implement strategies and use their own skills and abilities to the full.*

119

come to terms with the damage which can be caused (not all of which is the direct result of technological advance) appear to have outstripped its understanding of the results.

Antarctica again provides an excellent example. Just a few years ago the continent was effectively unscathed by human beings, but since the arrival of the scientific missions so much garbage has accumulated that each country's scientific station can be clearly identified by its waste. This may well be of relatively minor importance in the long term. After all, garbage can be cleared away and the landscape left unpolluted. But the practice of dumping garbage and, more importantly, of producing it, reflects an attitude which has to be addressed at all levels — an attitude moreover, which explains a development model based upon the maximisation of production, often at the expense of both people and the environment.

Any attitudinal change suggests the need for a definition of "the economy" which is far closer to Khor Kok Peng's "People's Economy" than to that in current economic textbooks. Changes along these lines would do much to advance the restructuring of the international economic order which Redclift and Porrit argue is necessary to achieve a more just world order and a sustainable development process underpinned by a spirit of partnership (as called for by the Brundtland Commission's report), and which forms the basis of the understanding of CAFOD and other NGOs. For, if development is to achieve the progress of people, it has to be carried out in a way which demonstrates a sense of mutual respect and facilitates the realisation of each individual's full human potential.

To sum up, the experience of the past 40 years has been both encouraging and disillusioning. While some people have seen an improvement in the quality of their lives, this improvement has been purchased at a potentially incalculable cost. The experience has revealed inherent weaknesses in the theory which has underpinned development practice, possibly because it has not placed people at the centre of the process. And, for this reason, it has called into question whether this practice can truly be named development. For development is not something which is done *to* people. But this is the approach which has been followed, whether its origins lie in the well-meaning efforts of foreign aid donors; in third world governments' jealous protection of their newly-independent sovereignty or their own position of power and privilege, in private industry's search for ever-increasing profits; or, possibly, in some combination of all three.

Eloquent testimony that this has been the case can be found in the many "cathedrals in the desert", to quote a recent speech by Britain's Minister for Overseas Development, Chris Patten (now the Minister for the Environment), which litter the history, not to mention the countryside, of third world development. And not all such "cathedrals" have been built by the official aid donors. NGOs too have attempted to make people the object of development, as the Mexican economist,

Gustavo Esteva, has pointed out. And far from receding, the possibility exists that some NGOs will build more such "cathedrals" in the future. There is some considerable urgency, then, that the meaning of development should be clarified if the process is not to become further discredited. For some both in the industrialised world and in the Third World, to the left and right of the political spectrum, it is already discredited. In Britain, for example, Lord Bauer argues from a right-wing perspective that aid is harmful and anti-developmental because it creates a hand-out mentality amongst the recipients and rewards governments for keeping their people in poverty. On the left, Teresa Hayter and others have argued that, since aid's purpose is to meet the needs of the industrialised world and maintain the present imbalance in the international economic system in favour of the North, it is anti-developmental and reproduces poverty in the Third World. Hayter believes that third world people would be better-off if they were left to develop themselves in their own way. Meanwhile, from the Third World, Gustavo Esteva has expressed the view that the recent global economic crisis is, perversely, to be welcomed because it has created the opportunity for third world countries and peoples to free themselves from the development delusion. Such views are those of a minority at present, but they might become a majority view if the process results in still further "cathedrals in the desert" in the future.

In what remains of this chapter, we shall attempt to draw out the strands of our understanding of development and its relationship to the environment. The conclusions reached will, of necessity, be tentative — no strategy can guarantee that mistakes will not be made in the future. But with further experience, greater understanding and clarity will result, and this will permit the evolution of a more definitive understanding of what development is.

i. *Investment in the future.* If real development is to take place it needs to be sustainable over a far longer timespan than that normally considered by development strategists and economists generally. This should not be taken to mean that, for example, a mine with a lifespan of 15 to 20 years should not be opened. On the contrary, there may well be reasons why opening such a mine and using it for its lifespan is not only desirable but also necessary for increasing a country's wealth. What it does mean is that a greater proportion of the wealth extracted from the mine should be used in such a way as to benefit the country's population as a whole. In other words, the mine and its operation should contribute to the country's future as well as its present viability. This may seem self-evident but, as we have seen in the case of the Marcopper Mining Corporation's operation in the Philippines, the Indonesian transmigration programme, or the many other instances involving pollution around the world, it frequently does not occur.

ii. *Wider and more numerous measurements.* A far wider set of measurements than is now available needs to be developed. For environmental activists like Redclift and Porrit, such measurements would have to include calculations of the cost of the loss of the use of certain finite resources at some future point in time, as well as of the almost incalculable costs of the loss of possible medicines or foods, not to mention the loss of genetic resources resulting from the destruction or severe degradation of tropical forests.

Similarly, one would have to find a way to calculate the costs of industrial pollution in both the present and future generations, to say nothing of its present and possible future impact on the local and global environment. It is fairly well recognised, for example, that the absorption of high mercury levels, particularly from fish, could result in both lower intelligence and higher levels of aggression in future generations. Similar findings have been made regarding the ingestion of other heavy metals, notably lead. As the Chernobyl disaster clearly showed, pollution — be it nuclear, as in this case, chemical or industrial — respects no international boundaries. Industrial pollution in all its forms is a subject of increasing international concern and the widespread recognition of the need to eradicate its causes is casting serious doubts on the chances of further industrialisation, regardless of where it occurs. What is certain is that the costs of any future industrialisation will have to increase significantly if forests are to be protected from acid rain, the threat posed by the greenhouse effect reduced and further destruction of the ozone layer prevented.

Accidents will occur but their risk can be minimised, not only through correct safety procedures, but also, and probably more importantly, through the adoption of correct policies. Thus it is clearly necessary that anti-pollution standards applicable in the industrialised world should also apply in the Third World. This is at best a minimal position but one which is ignored as a daily reality. Pictures of smog pollution in Mexico City are evocative of earlier pictures of London smog, and the reality is just as deadly for Mexicans as it was for Londoners. Similarly, some effective means of establishing and enforcing international standards in relation to pesticide use would appear to be necessary. As we have seen, the transfer of industrial agricultural models to third world countries has resulted in the pollution of third world water systems as well as those in industrialised countries, with possibly greater negative effects on nutrition in the Third World. Clearly, this is unacceptable.

Nor are these environmental concerns the limit of the new measurements which need to be developed. Development will have cultural, social and political as well as environmental and economic effects, and these are equally valid concerns for development planners. But this does not mean that such changes should be resisted. On the contrary, as we have seen in the discussion of the San people of southern Africa, conservation can have effects as negative as modernisation. Thus care should be exercised to maximise the positive aspects of a society's social, political and cultural heritage, thereby creating the conditions for its future vitality.

iii. *A change in attitudes*. The development of such policies calls for a major shift in the approach to economic growth. The discussion of the elements of Khor Kok Peng's "People's Economy" clearly identified at least some of the elements of this attitudinal change. Some level of growth is clearly both necessary and desirable. Better distribution of existing wealth will be inadequate to meet the needs of all the world's people in the immediate future, to say nothing of their longer-term needs and wants. Thus, it is important that the policies which are implemented provide not only for the sustainability of current standards of living but also for improvements in the quality of life. One way in which this could be achieved in the immediate future would be to make greater use of the resources already existing in the communities themselves. Thus, rather than overemphasising the construction of large dams, for example, there would be far more investment in improving already existing local alternatives such as ponds, weirs and so on.

Similarly, far more could be invested in the development of seeds adapted to local conditions, which would maximise production without the addition of expensive inputs. Increased recycling of waste material would similarly reduce the need for exploitation. Industrialised countries could learn a lot from third world societies, where little goes to waste and many people subsist by recovering usable items from rubbish tips. Goods produced could also be built to last longer. But, if this happens, then the prices of raw materials should reflect their real value, rather than their present unrealistically low levels.

iv. *Real partnership*. Communities in the Third World will have to identify their needs themselves and plan and implement strategies on the ground — which will demand a far greater degree of trust and a belief in their knowledge and abilities on the part of those who work with them. Development must be culturally specific and those who practise it or, equally importantly, assist in its practice should be sensitive to the cultures of the people with whom they work.

v. *Small-scale and large-scale development*. The successes which NGOs have achieved in the past have been on twofold. Firstly, they have stressed that development can only take place when the people of the area want it. This may seem self-evident, but much of the failure of large-scale projects can be put down to a sense of lack of ownership on the part of local people, so that, when the "experts" depart, the project falls by the wayside because nobody is willing to take on the responsibility for its maintenance.

Secondly, the approach would also appear to guarantee a high level of participation by the people themselves. Such participation not only reinforces a sense of ownership but also provides insurance against the possibility of ill-conceived projects or mistakes in their design. Local knowledge of the results of waterlogging resulting from over-irrigation may have gone some way to dissuade development planners from placing too great an emphasis on irrigation projects, for example. In essence, therefore, such an approach accords people their rightful place in the process — at the centre of their own development.

Nevertheless, there will inevitably be occasions when smaller-scale projects such as those outlined above will be totally inadequate to meet the needs of a country. Transport and communications are obvious examples. In these circumstances, the benefits of programmes have to be calculated in terms of their costs — both immediate and longer-term. And the planning of such large-scale projects should obviously involve the widest possible consultation with and participation by the people whom it will affect, so that they understand the potential benefits which will result.

For example, if a dam has to be constructed to guarantee power and water for irrigation, the people who will be displaced must be made aware of the planning from the earliest stage and be guaranteed not only compensation for the loss of their homes and land but also enough time to carry out their culturally necessary rituals, and so on. In short, communities affected by such projects should be provided with the time and support which they require to come to terms with their need to move and start again. Thus, it is possible, given the will, to ensure that people occupy their rightful position in their own and their countries' development.

Such a strategy is not a development panacea, the application of which will prevent mistakes in the future. Neither are the suggested

A community-based tree nursery in south-western Sri Lanka, under the direction of a young Buddhist monk. For successful development, it is essential that local people participate in projects and have a real sense of ownership.

Photo: Mark Edwards/Still Pictures

five points original insights. Their sense is endorsed by the Brundtland Commission's report[16], which also underlines the importance of participation and administrative flexibility (see points ii-v above). The commission further argues that economic policy should encourage self-reliance and sustainability, while technology itself should search continuously for new solutions (see points i and iii). Furthermore, the commission urged that production should respect the ecological base (points i and v), while the international system should be one which fosters sustainable patterns of trade and finance (point iii).

A place for practical idealism

Development is, ideally, a participatory continuum in which all parties — the people, their governments, foreign aid donors and experts and private enterprise — interact on a daily basis to the general benefit. It is not a process which results in short-term profit to the detriment of the future. Rather it is a process which guarantees future profits. Nor is it a static state which maintains the current situation or an approximation of the way things used to be in some "golden age" in the past. Development, like all living societies, is dynamic. It carries the best of the past into the future.

Within such a context, it is likely that communities which will be adversely affected initially by necessary large-scale development projects, will be willing to surrender some of their existing rights in return for future benefits. But this requires a conciliatory approach to conflict resolution, designed to limit, as far as possible, the cost to any single group in a society. Such an approach would do much to address the causes of past development failures, while creating the conditions in which those previously left out of the process can be incorporated. This would help to prevent future avoidable errors, for if it is the people themselves who identify their needs and work to see that they are met, they are also likely to be able to respond quickly to difficulties and problems which arise in implementation.

Furthermore, although they may not use phrases like sustainable or environmentally safe when they talk about development, what they do in practice is likely to be both those things. And where it is not, there are likely to be good reasons for this, which should be accepted in the spirit of partnership underlying the development process suggested. There is a danger of straying too far from people's needs in much of the critique originating in the environmental movement, which frequently seems to advocate conservation for its own sake.

Economic growth can occur within a framework of care for the environment, as we saw when discussing the work of the Green Belt Movement in Kenya, the efforts of the government and people of Cape Verde and the Mogoraib-Forto integrated development project. All three demonstrate this clearly; and the last does so even though a significant component of the project is improvement of the area's communications through the construction of a road network. Such undertakings have long been the *bête noire* of the environmental movement, as have parts of the development movement, who have argued that they do little to benefit the local population.

Undoubtedly, this criticism has been justified on occasion. As we saw in *Land and Poverty*, the Trans-Amazonia highway in Brazil did little to benefit either *posseiros* (peasant farmers) in the area through which the road passed, or the Brazilian Amerindians. But this is a comment not on the fact that a road was constructed, but on the way in which it was planned and built, as well as the motivation behind it. It may be that had the Brazilian government and the aid donors funding the road's construction followed the suggestions outlined above, the outcome would have been very different — perhaps a railway might have been built instead. Certainly, the road's ultimate purpose would have been different. Furthermore, it is questionable whether the experience of the country's Amerindians would have been so universally negative.

Ultimately, development must be for people. And the process by which it is achieved should be consultative and participatory — if regrettably, but unavoidably, slow. This is not to suggest that third world people should be condemned to their present quality of life for the foreseeable future. On the contrary, haste in creating the conditions for improved living standards is of the essence. But if development is to be of the kind which permits people everywhere to realise their full human potential, it should follow the maxim "more haste, less speed".

Notes

16. *Our Common Future: Report of the World Commission on Environment and Development*, pp.43-66, Oxford University Press (Oxford, 1987).

THE WORLD BANK'S POLICY ON INTEGRATING ENVIRONMENTAL ISSUES INTO DEVELOPMENT STRATEGIES

Before the recent reorganisation instituted under the new president, Barber Conable, the World Bank tried to address environmental concerns through the small Office of Environmental and Scientific Affairs, which was established in 1972, making the institution the first multilateral development bank to set up an environmental unit. This indication of the Bank's theoretical commitment was underlined in 1980 when it signed the Declaration of the Committee on Integrated Development Institutions and the Environment (CIDIE). There were three staff qualified in environmental areas at this stage, and the emphasis of their work was on the environmental impact of individual projects. Staff in other units of the Bank with a background or personal interest in environmental issues also provided support, which helped to broaden environmental activities somewhat.

Activities under this heading were stated to include: (a) making operational staff aware of ecological, cultural and resource management concerns; (b) participating in operational missions to address through design, redesign or remedial action any negative environmental aspects of projects; (c) developing environmental projects; (d) co-operating with the United Nations Development Programme on plans to assess environmental issues in a number of countries; and (e) jointly sponsoring with the United Nations Environment Programme a series of workshops on national accounting for the environment. The Bank's operational manual on internal procedures urged all Bank staff to attend to the integration of environmental concerns in country economic and sector work. Guidelines in this area were expanded and made more specific, and reviews of compliance were initiated. However, owing to the small number of environmental staff, these efforts were largely inadequate.

In April 1987, the Bank presented a paper, *Environment, Growth and Development*, to the Development Committee which comprises the representatives of member countries. This paper presented the views then current within the Bank on environmental matters. It covered the inter-relationship between economic growth, poverty alleviation and environmental degradation and emphasised the importance of addressing environmental issues in the context of overall economic policy, rather than simply by concern with individual projects. It recommended that relevant work should be carried out by developing member countries, the Bank and the rest of the development community and expressly stated that, while work on individual projects

127

was essential, it was also inadequate and should be supplemented by explicitly building environmental concerns into all aspects of development.

An increased emphasis on environmental work has been an important element both during the Bank's reorganisation and since its completion in 1988. Environmental units have been established in all four regions, and a Central Environmental Department has been set up in the Senior Vice-Presidency for Policy, Planning and Research. The Bank now says it pursues the following objectives: (a) integrating environmental concerns more actively and systematically in country economic and sector work and lending operations; while, at the same time, (b) continuing to assess the impact of projects financed by the Bank in order to minimise negative environmental consequences.

It is stated that these objectives will be met as follows:

Environmental issues papers. Towards the latter end of 1989, the department plans to have completed an environmental issues paper for each borrowing country as a contribution to the planning of country economic and sector work. Where the issues are considered sufficiently important, a formal environmental issues meeting will be held to discuss the paper. Subjects which require special attention will be identified, and a scheme of actions proposed. Subsequent issues papers will be designed to monitor progress, update information, and propose new, or modified, programmes.

Country studies. About 30 countries will also be chosen for in-depth analysis of selected, key environmental issues within countries and regions over a five-year period, with assistance from UNDP and bilateral donors. In essence, the studies are intended to provide a review of the extent and severity of environmental degradation, its immediate and underlying causes, as well as developing policies and investment programmes to improve environmental management.

Lending operations. It is expected that this policy emphasis will lead to an increase in the number of Bank project loans and structural or sector adjustment loans which include support for environmental management as a component. Increased efforts will also be made to identify opportunities for loans for straightforward environmental projects.

Project review. All relevant documentation at each stage of a project funding cycle will be reviewed by the relevant regional environment unit, which will alert the country department and sector operations staff to the need for measures to avoid or remedy negative environmental consequences.

Training. A training programme for operational staff, in both sector and country operations units, will alert them to the need for such measures.

The Bank says it is fully aware of the time involved in environmental work and its complex effects. Together with its acknowledgement of its relative shortage of staff with ecological and anthropological skills, this means it accepts the need to rely heavily on outside consultants to implement its policies. The Bank also seemingly recognises that the moves taken so far are no more than a starting point in the necessary process of developing a programme of environmental management. Thus, the possible staffing and budgetary implications of the new policy direction have been acknowledged.

Source: World Bank Procedures for Integrating Environmental Issues into Country Strategies, ODA, October 1987.

BRITISH AID AND THE ENVIRONMENT TO 1989

Since the UN Conference on the Human Environment in 1972, Britain's Overseas Development Administration (ODA) has been committed, on paper at least, to the avoidance of serious and irreversible environmental damage in its promotion of economic development, and has aimed to improve the overall quality of the atmosphere, of water sources and of life itself. This commitment was underlined by the Minister for Overseas Development in a speech to the Overseas Development Council in Washington, on 7 June 1988. Mr Patten explained ODA's commitment to care for the environment, saying it was "no longer a luxury for fringe lobby groups, but an implacable necessity if large groups of poor people struggling for existence in an increasingly fragile environment are to survive".

The government's commitment to "the concept of *sustainable economic development*" (emphasis in original) was further underlined by the Prime Minister in a speech to the Royal Society on 27 September 1988. Mrs Thatcher told the society that "stable prosperity can be achieved throughout the world provided the environment is nurtured and safeguarded". Britain's aid policy, therefore, was one of the first to respond to the growing international concern at the environmental impact of economic development.

However, during the 1987/88 financial year ODA began to develop detailed guidelines, which at the time of writing (December 1988) had only just been published for comment.[17] The lack of detailed guidelines should not suggest that ODA staff operated in a policy vacuum. Guidance was most recently provided in August 1981 by the official *Policy Guidance Note* (PGN No 24) together with annexes offering a checklist for screening environmental aspects in aid activities (Annex 6 to III — A-2).

PGN 24 starts from the understanding that part of the very purpose of development is to disturb the environment, because development aims to utilise "resources more intensively, or in a different place, or in different combinations, so that people may have more or better food or drink, clothing, shelter, education, health, employment, opportunities for a better life". It is clearly acknowledged that this disturbance can be both positive and negative — for example, projects to restore the environment destroyed by other processes, such as soil erosion — but the note recognises that, in the majority of cases, project finance requests will have environmental implications more complex than they originally appear. In these circumstances, ODA policy requires that project appraisal studies should incorporate a description of such indirect effects including, where possible "without inordinate expense", their likely cost.

Decision as to what constitutes "inordinate expense" is left to the geographical department or the development division responsible for the project but these are enjoined to consult with the environmental adviser where there is doubt. Ultimately, however, such decisions have an impact on the available funds, as expert assessment has to be commissioned from outside the ODA in the overwhelming majority of cases. Thus, responsible desk officers are likely to exercise caution in calling for such non-departmental expert assistance, as it will reduce the funds available for the actual programme.

Possibly because of this, PGN 24 explicitly states that projects which involve:

● substantial changes in land use (eg the introduction of forestry, arable or bush fallow farming or human settlements where they have not previously been);

● substantial changes in water use (eg irrigation, water supplies);

● substantial changes in farming or fishing practice (eg use of pesticides and fertilisers, introduction of new crops, mechanisation);

● major infrastructure (eg dams, ports);

● industrial processes generating toxic waste (eg pulp mills, chemical plants, mining);

● changes in fragile environments (small islands, thinly or densely populated areas, arid areas);

● resource recycling, energy and nutrient conservation, waste management, "ought to be considered in depth" so that their environmental impact can be assessed. In the same vein, all projects involving "wildlife conservation or nature reserves, whether with or without tourist development" should be referred to the environmental adviser as a matter of course.

PGN 24 is clear that ODA's concern for the environmental impact of a project does not mean that it is able to force third world governments to take this into account. However, it observes that "ODA can and should explain the options and their implications, so that at least the choice made is a conscious one; and it is of course open to ODA not to support a choice with which it disagrees". But there are clearly occasions when ODA will accept levels of environmental damage. The note observes that "acceptance of the importance of the environment involves concern for *sustainable* benefits, which may have to be weighed against greater short term but *unsustainable* benefits" (original emphasis). This implicitly accepts that, on occasion at least, the short-term potential benefits of a project outweigh its sustainability over time.

It is also stressed that potential environmental effects should be dealt with in "the planning and appraisal of any project in which they are likely to be important".

Annex 6 sets out an extensive, and admittedly incomplete, check list to help guide those involved in the preparation, approval, implementation and monitoring of activities in the relevant sectors. It is perhaps worth listing the environmental areas on which advice "should be" sought on receipt of proposals affecting them:

i. National parks, nature reserves and all other areas designated for conservation of wildlife and landscape features.

ii. Areas containing endangered species of plant and animal.

iii. Tropical and sub-tropical forests (including mangroves).

iv. Coral reefs.

v. Wetlands.

Notes

17. The final version was published under the title *Manual of Environmental Appraisal* in March 1989. Asked to comment on a draft version, the members of the informal Aid and Environment Group of British NGOs welcomed the many improvements it contained but pointed to four areas of particular concern: the terms of the aid-trade provision, the failure to define environmentally unacceptable projects, the lack of sufficient "Brundtland" orientation and the possibility that the manual's very existence might marginalise the issue.

Glossary

Acid rain. Term used to describe fallout of industrial pollutants, sometimes literally as acidified rainfall and sometimes as dry deposition. Most of these pollutants come from burning fossil fuels or from vehicle exhausts. Acid rain damages trees, crops and plants; acidifies lakes, rivers and groundwater; and corrodes buildings.

Agrarian reform. The distribution of land more equally throughout the population, together with equitable access to credit and extension services. Many see agrarian reform as a critical component of effective agricultural development, although the initial impact is often to disrupt production temporarily.

Balance of payments. That part of a nation's accounts showing international transactions, usually over an annual period. It highlights the difference between money raised and money paid out both as a result of direct financial transfers and the money value of all international activity like foreign trade, travel, freight and insurance.

Bilateral aid. The term used to describe official aid allocated directly by the donor to the recipient country.

Biocide. Literally "life-killing". A term applied to those chemicals used to destroy living organisms which interfere with or threaten human health and activities. Biocides include: herbicides (weeds); insecticides (insect pests); nematicides (eelworms and similar); acaricides (mites); fungicides (plant diseases and moulds) and rodenticides (rats, mice). Some biocides are selective, being most potent against a small number of species, but others are more generally toxic. The term pesticide is more generally used in place of biocide.

Biogas. A methane-rich gas produced by the fermentation of animal dung and human dung, or crop residues, and used as fuel or as fertiliser in many developing countries.

Biomass. Scientific term used to describe the dry animal and plant matter found on the face of the planet.

Biotechnology. A generic term for those technologies that seek to use living organisms (or parts of) to modify existing forms of life or to generate new life; the application of biological organisms, systems or processes to manufacturing industry.

Brundtland Commission. Popular name given to the World Commission on Environment and Development chaired by Mrs Gro Harlem Brundtland, Prime Minister of Norway. Its report, *Our Common Future*, is similarly often referred to as the "Brundtland Report".

Chlorofluorocarbons (CFC's). Chlorine-based compounds used as aerosol propellants, refrigerants, coolants, sterilants, solvents and in the production of foam packaging used by the fast-food industry. There is no natural mechanism for the removal of CFC's from the lower atmosphere — they only break down under the action of ultraviolet light when they enter the upper atmosphere. They are environmentally dangerous on two accounts: they are greenhouse gases, trapping the earth's radiation before it can escape into space and thus heating the planet through the "greenhouse effect"; they also release chlorine as they break down, which reacts with ozone and destroys the ozone layer above the earth.

Commodities. The term used to describe the agricultural and/or mineral commodities or products produced by a given country. The South is still heavily dependent on the production and export of these basic commodities — indeed, some developing countries obtain almost all their export earnings from just one commodity.

Comparative advantage. The idea, first advanced by economist David Ricardo, that economic agents are most effectively employed in activities in which they perform *relatively* better than in others. The importance of comparative advantage in international trade is that it suggests that even if a country is very bad at some activity — perhaps worse than any other country — it could still be efficient for it to pursue this activity if it is even more inept at other activities.

Debt service. Repayment, composed of interest and capital, due in respect of a loan. A debt service ratio is the ratio of foreign debt service payments to earnings from exports.

Desertification. The term used to describe the increase of desert land as a result of human action (as opposed to desertisation, which refers to the natural process by which deserts increase). Desertification is the final stage in the slow and insidious process of land degradation, which starts with the loss of vegetative cover and ends with the destruction of the soil's fertility and its transformation into barren desert. The most vulnerable soils are to be found in the tropics.

Developing countries. Sometimes referred to as less developed countries. There is no single standard definition. The Organisation for Economic Co-operation and Development's Development Assistance Committee produced a list of developing countries originally as a guide for its members' statistical reporting, but it has since acquired a certain international significance. The list includes all countries in Africa, except South Africa; all countries in America, except the USA and Canada; all countries in Asia except Japan; and all countries in Oceania, except Australia and New Zealand. In Europe the list includes Cyprus, Gibraltar, Greece, Malta, Portugal, Turkey and Yugoslavia. There are other lists in international use and all differ slightly.

Donor. A country, either developed or developing, providing assistance to a developing country, either directly or through a multilateral agency.

Economic growth. An increase in the country's total output. This may be measured by the annual rate of increase in a country's Gross National Product (GNP) or Gross Domestic Product (GDP), as adjusted for price changes. An increase in GNP merely indicates the average level of living within a country, but says nothing about the distribution of this wealth throughout the different social groups in that society.

Ecosystem. A community of organisms and their interrelated physical and chemical environment. It can apply equally to a geographical area of land or ocean, or to the entire planet.

Environmental sustainability. A quality of a management system which guarantees: the maintenance of essential ecosystem processes; the maintenance of biological diversity and all important species in each local ecosystem; the maintenance of harvests at levels which do not jeopardise sustainable yields in the future; and the satisfaction of the needs of local people.

Erosion. The removal of soil due to the action of wind and rain. Under natural conditions, erosion is an extremely slow process, but as a result of deforestation, overgrazing and inappropriate farming practices, the earth's topsoil is now being eroded at an alarming rate.

European Development Fund (EDF). The instrument of financial and technical co-operation between the European Community and the African, Caribbean and Pacific (ACP) states which are signatories to the Lomé Conventions. Each convention has a separate EDF. All community members contribute to the Fund, which is effectively administered by the European Commission.

First World. The developed world: the West, Japan and developed Oceania (Australia and New Zealand).

General Agreement on Tariffs and Trade (GATT). This is the principal international institution devoted to the achievement of a reduction in trade barriers and an expansion in world trade. Established in 1947, it operates by voluntary agreement of member trading nations. Under GATT rules, special provision is made for developing countries which, within certain limits, are not required to reduce their trade barriers to the same extent as the participating industrialised countries.

Genetic engineering. The transfer of genes between organisms of different species.

Genetic resources. The genetic variability of the natural world, constituting a major resource base, with wild plants and animals providing a huge potential for new crops, medicines, fibres and food.

Greenhouse effect. Growing levels of carbon dioxide in the atmosphere (released by the burning of fossil fuels — coal, oil, gas, firewood etc) form a blanket around the earth, holding in much of the solar radiation which would otherwise escape into space. This is resulting in a gradual warming of the atmosphere (1°C in the last 150 years), known as the "greenhouse" effect.

Green revolution. Launched as a result of the UN FAO World Food Congress in 1963 and its Freedom from Hunger Campaign, it aimed to combat the projected food needs of the growing population and to produce sufficient food to bring an end to hunger. Formally known as the Indicative Plan for Agricultural Development, it involved the introduction of high-yielding cereal varieties developed in the Philippines. These cereals had short stems, to avoid being blown over by the wind, and were quick-maturing, making three crops possible on the same land in one year. The food quality of the hybrids is lower; they are vulnerable to moulds, thus difficult to store; they are vulnerable to pests and diseases, thus requiring massive application of pesticides; they require irrigation water; and they provide high-yields only when used in conjunction with heavy application of fertilisers. The huge costs required to use these varieties effectively led small farmers into debt; others went out of business; large agribusiness moved in. The costs involved also helped to escalate Third World debt, necessitating the export of the food which was produced from these varieties.

Gross Domestic Product (GDP). GDP is the total value of goods and services produced within a country in a given year.

Gross National Product (GNP). GNP is equal to GDP plus the income generated abroad by a country's nationals or companies in a given year but less similar payments made to other countries.

Inter-American Development Bank (IADB). One of the four regional development banks. Established in 1959 to promote the development of member countries through financial assistance and technical co-operation, its membership was originally restricted to the states in the Organisation of American States (OAS). This was extended to include Canada in 1976, and later to allow 12 other countries to join as non-regional members; others have since joined in this way. Funds are replenished every four years.

International Monetary Fund (IMF). Institution set up, together with the World Bank, its sister body, at the Bretton Woods Conference in 1945. Its purpose was to promote international monetary co-operation and the expansion of international trade, to facilitate monetary convertability and to ensure financial stability. The IMF is an international body with 140 members; in practice, power is exercised by the five members with the largest quota: the UK, USA, West Germany, Japan and France. The IMF is primarily the lender of the last resort to third world governments that are in balance of payments difficulties. Debtor governments can borrow up to the limit of their special drawing rights (SDR) in exchange for their own currency; if they wish to borrow more they must accept IMF conditions. These conditions include reducing expenditure (particularly "non-productive" expenditure, such as health, welfare, education and food subsidies); reducing real wages; the expansion of cash-cropping for export at the expense of domestic production of food; and currency devaluation. Critics of these "structural adjustment policies" point out that it is the poor who are hardest hit by these reforms.

Life expectancy. Most figures refer to life expectancy at birth. This indicates the number of years newborn children are likely to live, subject to the mortality risks prevailing for the cross section of the population at the time of their birth. In 1987 the world's average newborn child could expect to live 61 years, whereas ten years earlier the average child could have expected a life-span of only 55 years.

Less Developed Countries (LDCs). Broad category covering all developing countries. Not to be confused with Least Developed Countries (LLDCs), the UN category of 37 developing countries which are low-income commodity exporters with low industrial bases.

Multi-Fibre Arrangement (MFA). A set of quotas and other trade restrictions to limit the growth of textile imports into the EC from countries of the South, apart from most of those associated with the EC through the Lomé Convention (a trade and aid agreement between the EC and 66 countries of Africa, the

Caribbean and the Pacific) and certain Mediterranean and East European countries. It is made under the provision of GATT for Safeguards on Imports. In the South, imports from those countries that are restricted by the MFA have grown more slowly than those from European countries outside the community, while imports from the US (not in MFA) — the single largest exporter to the EC — rose by 65% between 1978 and 1979.

Multilateral aid. This is official foreign aid that is channelled through international agencies like the World Bank, the EEC and the different bodies of the United Nations.

Newly-industrialised countries. Those Southern countries which enjoyed a rapid growth of manufacturing output and are now significant exporters of manufactured goods. They are located, in the main, in South-East Asia and in Latin America.

Non-governmental organisations (NGOs). Sometimes called the voluntary agencies. Private organisations of a charitable, research or educational nature concerning themselves with the problems of the Third World and the spread of knowledge about them. Some collect funds from the public to undertake development projects or disaster relief; other activities include research into development issues.

North/South. The North is shorthand for the industrialised developed countries of the world, including those within the Soviet bloc. The South is shorthand for the poorer, developing, third world countries.

Organisation for African Unity (OAU). Established in 1963, the OAU is an association of some 50 African countries. It operates to promote unity and solidarity among African countries through co-ordinated efforts in the fields of politics, diplomacy, economics, health and education. It is pledged in particular to eliminate all forms of colonialism, including apartheid, from the continent. Its statutes forbid interference in the internal affairs of member countries.

Organisation for Economic Co-operation and Development (OECD). Set up in 1961 to replace the Organisation for European Economic Co-operation (OEEC), it comprises the 20 major Western economies. Its headquarters are in Paris. Its objectives include promoting policies to achieve the highest sustainable levels of economic growth and employment in member countries, thereby also contributing to the development of the world economy.

Overgrazing. The overstocking of land with grazing stock can all but eliminate plant cover, particularly when the animals are clustered in small areas, such as a waterhole, or kept on the same land for a long period. Eventually the land is laid bare. The soil is then vulnerable to erosion and ultimately desertification. Overgrazing is now fairly common throughout the dry tropics, especially where traditional pastoralism has been replaced by intensive livestock-rearing schemes. Traditional pastoralists avoided the problem by ranging excessively over large areas.

Overseas Development Association (ODA). That part of the British Civil Service with overall responsibility for the official British Aid programmes. It is part of the Foreign and Commonwealth Office, but prior to the 1979 general election was a separate ministry called the Overseas Development Ministry (ODM).

Ozone layer. A layer of pale blue gas (of the oxygen family) in the earth's stratosphere, which protects us from the ultraviolet radiation from the sun.

Pesticides. A term used more or less as a synonym for biocides.

Primary health care. Community-based strategy for health for all, involving health monitoring and education.

Programme aid. That part of official aid which is provided as support for vital imports, usually to assist countries with particularly acute balance of payments problems.

Project aid. Grants or loans to finance the establishment of new (or to expand existing) production and infrastructure facilities such as hydro-electric plants, railway expansion, equipment for educational schemes etc. In other words, it is tied to specific projects or investments.

Regional Development Banks (RDBs). Smaller versions of the World Bank, the RDBs' capital is subscribed from member countries in the same way as the World Bank's, and they lend for the same purposes and on similar terms. They are independent of the World Bank, although they sometimes work with it on specific projects. The four RDBs are: the Inter-American Development Bank; the African Development Bank; the Asian Development Bank; the Arab Fund for Economic and Social Development.

Salinisation. When land is too salty to support plant life it is said to be salinised. Although salinisation does occur naturally, increasingly land is being rendered saline through human activity, the chief culprit being perennial irrigation schemes. Salinisation occurs when the delicate salt balance of the soil is upset, thus allowing salts to build up in the root zone of crops or, worse still, to form a saline crust on the surface. Perennial irrigation schemes — where land is irrigated year after year without ever being left fallow — are the major cause of salinisation in dry/arid areas. Unless the land is well-drained, irrigation inevitably causes the water-table to rise, bringing the salt to the surface.

Sharecroppers. Tenant farmers who pay part of their crop as rent.

Structural adjustment. The process by which economies change or are forced to change their basic structures through a reallocation of resources and initiated principally because of balance of payments difficulties.

Sub-Saharan Africa. A term most commonly used to describe all the countries of Africa apart from those north of the Sahara desert and South Africa. The northern African countries usually excluded from SSA are Algeria, Egypt, Libya, Morocco and Tunisia and Western Sahara.

Sustainable development. As outlined by the Brundtland Commission sustainable development is: "development that meets the needs of the present without compromising the ability of future generations to meet their own needs."

Third World. Less developed countries (the South).

Trickle-down development. The theory of development by which investment at the top, in industry and high-technology projects, creates wealth which will "trickle-down" to the poor.

United Nations Children's Fund (UNICEF). A specialised UN agency established by the UN General Assembly in 1946, on a temporary basis, for relief work in war-devastated areas. Its mandate was extended in 1953 for an indefinite period. Its purpose is to assist in combating widespread malnutrition, disease and illiteracy affecting millions of children principally in the Third World, through both emergency and longer-term programmes of assistance. It is financed entirely by voluntary contributions from governments, private groups and individuals.

United Nations Conference on Trade and Development (UNCTAD). A permanent organ of the UN General Assembly, set up in 1964 and based in Geneva. It has over 160 countries as members. Its main function is to promote and *monitor international trade, especially with a view to accelerating the economic development of poorer countries. The Conference generally meets formally every four years.

United Nations Development Decade. The UN designated Development Decades in order to focus on developing countries and to accelerate the development of their human and natural resources by effective international action. The first Development Decade was from 1961 to 1970. We are currently approaching the start of the fourth.

United Nations Development Programme (UNDP). In 1966 the UN Special Fund and the Expanded Programme of Technical Assistance were merged under this new title to assist by providing research, training, resources and expertise in programmes of technical co-operation (i.e. not ordinary development capital). Funds for UNDP are provided by voluntary contributions of UN member governments.

United Nations Environment Programme (UNEP). Established as a result of the UN Conference on the Human Environment in Stockholm, 1972, UNEP promotes international co-operation in the environment field and acts as a forum for the co-ordination of environmental action within the UN system. UN administers the UN Environment Fund, a voluntary fund to provide additional finance for environmental programmes or projects.

United Nations Food and Agricultural Organisation (FAO). Based in Rome and set up in 1945, this specialised UN agency exists to promote the improved production and distribution of food and to raise nutritional and living standards of the people of its member countries. It is also concerned with famine and food-deficit problems; it has set up Early Warning Systems and was co-sponsor (with the UN) of the World Food Programme set up in 1963 to use food commodities, cash and services to back programmes of development and provide emergency relief for the victims of disaster. FAO policies have been criticised for insisting on the mechanisation of agriculture, the maximising of the use of fertilisers and encouraging the increase in land under perennial irrigation. Its three committees on agriculture, fisheries and forestry currently represent the only inter-governmental fora where major problems relating to these areas can be examined and discussed on a global basis.

United States Agency for International Development (USAID). The official bilateral donor agency of the US government.

Water-borne diseases. Diseases transmitted by bacteria, insects and other organisms that live or breed in water. Examples include cholera, schistosomiasis (*bilharzia*), malaria, river blindness, diarrhoea, leprosy, yellow fever, trachoma, scabies, polio and elephantiasis. Such diseases kill an estimated 25,000 people a day. In urban areas lack of pollution controls, particularly from sewage outlets and industrial plants, are a major cause of gastro-intestinal disease in third world countries. In rural areas dams and other water projects, notably irrigation programmes, have played a major role in spreading schistosomiasis, malaria and other diseases.

World Bank. The Washington-based financial lending institution set up after the Bretton Woods conference in 1944. It is the term now commonly used for three distinct though interrelated bodies housed at the World Bank headquarters. The largest is the International Bank for Reconstruction and Development (IBRD), which lends to governments of third world countries that are considered creditworthy and to agencies of those countries that have government guarantees against such borrowing. As the Bank borrows on the international financial markets, its interest rates are almost on a par with commercial rates, although the pay-back periods tend to be longer. The Bank's International Development Association (IDA) lends to poorer countries on highly-concessional terms. Its third arm, the International Finance Corporation (IFC) lends without government guarantees and takes equity shares in private sector enterprises in the Third World. The Bank is funded by subscriptions from its member states, grants to the IDA by the wealthier nations, loans and bonds raised on the world money markets, and the flow of repayments on its loans. The Bank is controlled by its member countries, whose votes are in accordance with the size of their respective contributions. This means that the World Bank is largely controlled by the United States, the largest donor.

World Commission of Environment and Development (the "Brundtland Commission"). An independent commission set up by the UN General Assembly in 1983 with the brief to give recommendations for a global agenda for change. Critical issues on the interlinked crises of the environment and development were to be examined and analysed. Guidelines for concrete and remedial action were to be proposed. Specifically, a strategy was to be formulated which would allow "sustainable development" to be achieved by the year 2000. Chaired by Mrs Gro Harlem Brundtland, Prime Minister of Norway, the commission was composed of 21 prominent figures and leaders in the fields of environment and development from around the world. The commission's report, *Our Common Future*, was published in 1987 and put forward 22 new legal principles to help achieve sustainable development, recommending that they be incorporated into national laws and into a world convention on the sovereign rights and duties of all nations. Policy-makers were to be guided by eight major interdependent goals:
● the revival of economic growth;
● an improvement in the quality of growth, ensuring environmental and social soundness, and meeting needs for jobs, food, energy, water and sanitation;
● the conservation and enhancement of the natural resource base;
● the stabilisation of population levels;
● the reorientation of technology and improved risk management;
● the integration of the environment and economics in decision making;
● the reformation of global economic relations; and
● a strengthening of international co-operation.

World Health Organisation (WHO). A specialised UN agency to help control disease and increase the general standards of health and nutrition through international co-operation. WHO sponsors research and promotes higher standards of teaching and training in the health and medical professions. Most of its work is based in developing countries, where tropical diseases are widespread, and where diseases eliminated from the First World still prevail.

World Resources Institute (WRI). The Washington-based research and policy centre to help governments, international organisations and the private sector and others to address the question of how societies can best meet human needs and nurture economic growth while preserving and sustainably managing the resource base and the environment as a whole. Produces policy studies and provides information on global resources and environmental conditions. In developing countries WRI also provides field studies and technical support for governments and NGOs. It is funded by the UN, government agencies, private foundations and individuals.

Select Bibliography

Advocates for African Food Security, *Case Studies from Africa: Towards Food Security*, UN Non-government Liaison Service (New York).

Agarwal, Bina, *Cold Hearths and Barren Slopes: The Woodfuel Crisis in the Third World*, Zed Books (London, 1986).

Bull, David, *A Growing Problem: Pesticides and the Third World Poor*, Oxfam (Oxford, 1982).

CAFOD, *Debt and Poverty* (London, 1987).

CAFOD, *Just Food* (London, 1984).

CAFOD, *Land and Poverty* (London, 1987).

Catholic Bishops Conference of the Philippines, *The Cry of Our Land*, pastoral letter of the National Secretariat for Social Action (1988).

Centre for Science and the Environment, *Citizens' report on the Environment*, (New Delhi).

Dankelman, Irene & Davidson, Joan (eds.), *Women and Environment in the Third World: Alliance for the Future*, Earthscan (London, 1988).

Dembo, David, *et al* (eds.), *Nothing to Lose But Our Lives: Empowerment to Oppose Industrial Hazards in a Transnational World*, Arena (Hong Kong, 1987).

Department of the Environment, *Our Common Future: A Perspective by the United Kingdom on the Report of the World Commission on Environment and Development*, DOE (London, July 1988).

Elkington, John, *Double Dividends: US Biotechnology and Third World Development*, World Resources Institute (Washington, 1986).

Elkington, John, *The Gene Factory: Inside the Biotechnology Business*, Century (London, 1985).

George, Susan, *A Fate Worse Than Debt*, Pelican (London, 1988).

Grainger, Alan, *Desertification: How People Make Deserts, How People Can Stop and Why They Don't*, Earthscan (London, 1982).

Harrison, Paul, *The Greening of Africa: Breaking Through in the Battle for Land and Food*, Paladin (London, 1987).

Higgot, Richard, *Political Development Theory*, Croom Helm (London, 1983).

Hill, Tony, (ed.), *Voices From Africa*, UN Non-government Liaison Service (Geneva, 1989).

Hobbelink, Henk, *New Hope or False Promise: Biotechnology and Third World Agriculture*, International Coalition for Development Action (Brussels, 1987).

Independent Commission on International Humanitarian Issues, *Indigenous Peoples: A Global Quest for Justice*, Zed Books (London, 1987).

Independent Commission on International Humanitarian Issues, *The Vanished Forest: The Human Consequences of Deforestation*, Zed Books (London, 1986).

Jackson, Tony & Eade, Deborah, *Against the Grain: The Dilemma of Food Aid*, Oxfam (Oxford, 1982).

Lamb, Robert, *World Without Trees*, Magnum (London, 1980).

MacAndrews, Colin, & Sien, Chia Lin (eds.), *Developing Economies and the Environment: The South-East Asian Experience*, McGraw-Hill (Singapore, 1979).

McAuslan, Patrick, *Urban Land and Shelter for the Poor*, Earthscan (London, 1985).

Mooney, P.R., *Seeds of the Earth: A Private or Public Resource?* International Coalition for Development Action (London).

Overseas Development Administration, *Manual of Environmental Appraisal*, ODA (London, March 1989).

Overseas Development Administration, *Policy Guidance Note No.24*, ODA (London, August 1981).

Overseas Development Administration, *World Bank Procedures for Integrating Environmental Issues into Country Strategies*, ODA (London, 1987).

Overseas Development Institute, *The Rich and the Poor: Changes in Incomes of Developing Countries Since 1960*, ODI briefing paper (London, June 1989).

Peng, Khor Kok, *Malaysia's Economy in Decline: What Happened? Why? What to do?* Consumers' Association of Penang (Penang, 1987).

Porritt, Jonathan, *Seeing Green: The Politics of Ecology Explained*, Blackwell (Oxford, 1987).

Redclift, Michael & Porritt, Jonathan, *Why Bankrupt the Earth? An Exploration into International Economics and the Environment*, The Other Economic Summit (1986).

Shiva, Vandana, *Forestry Crisis and Forestry Myths. A Critical Review of Tropical Rainforests: A Call for Action*, World Rainforest Movement (Penang, 1987).

Survival International, "Conserving Bushmen to Extinction in Southern Africa" in *An End to Laughter: Tribal Peoples and Economic Development*, Survival International Review, No.44 (1985).

Timberlake, Lloyd, *Africa in Crisis: The Causes, the Cures of Environmental Bankruptcy*, Earthscan (London, 1985).

Twose, Nigel, *Fighting the Famine*, Pluto Press (London, 1985).

United Nations Childrens' Fund, *The State of the World's Children*, Oxford University Press (Oxford, various years).

United Nations Conference on Trade and Development, *Trade and Development Report*, United Nations (New York, various years).

Ward, Barbara & Dubois, Rene, *Only One Earth: The Care and Maintenance of a Small Planet*, Pelican (London, 1972).

Wijkman, Anders & Timberlake, Lloyd, *Natural Disasters: Acts of God or Acts of Man?*, Earthscan (London, 1984).

Wisner, Ben, *Power and Need in Africa: Basic Human Needs and Development Policies*, Earthscan (London, 1988).

World Bank, *Accelerated Development in Sub-Saharan Africa* (the "Berg Report"), Oxford University Press (Oxford, 1981).

World Bank, *Environment, Growth and Development*, paper to development committee (Washington, 1987).

World Bank, *World Development Report*, Oxford University Press (Oxford, various years).

World Commission on Environment and Development, *Our Common Future*, Oxford University Press (Oxford, 1987).

World Development Movement, *Brundtland in the Balance: A Critique of the UK Government's Response to the World Commission on Environment and*

Development, WDM (London, February 1987).

World Resources Institute, *Tropical Rainforests: A Call for Action*, WRI (Washington, DC, 1985).

Index